Rich & Radiant

The High-Performing Woman's Guide to Freedom, Fulfillment, and a New Definition of Wealth

LIZ CARROLL

Liz Carroll-- 1st ed.
Chief Editor, Shannon Buritz
ISBN: 978-1-954757-71-4
Remarkable Press

I dedicate this book to my mom and all the women who share their stories with me.

CONTENTS

INTRODUCTION

What if you could feel rich and radiant before your bank account reflected it? What if the deep sense of calm confidence that lets you breathe easier and move through life without money constantly weighing on your mind was available to you right now?

Many high-achieving women live with a quiet undercurrent of worry. They've accomplished so much, yet they still feel stuck, isolated, or uncertain about what's next. They're earning well, but something feels off. The numbers might add up on paper, but emotionally, something isn't clicking. They crave clarity, direction, and a plan that actually feels good to follow.

I help women go from scarcity thinking—those negative loops that whisper *"you're behind"* or *"you should be doing more"*—to a mindset rooted in abundance and trust. When you can see your own forward movement and understand that you have the tools to handle whatever comes your way, something shifts. You stop worrying about "getting there" and start walking more surefooted, knowing that you've got your own back.

The goal is to have a financial plan that is flexible and adaptable to your real life, your evolving priorities, and your current circumstances. It's the difference between following outdated turn-by-turn directions and navigating with a sense of direction. You know where you're going, you understand the terrain, and even if it takes longer than you thought, you trust that you'll arrive exactly where you're meant to be.

You already know more than you think you do. You just need a guide to help you see it, name it, and act on it with intention. Because what's been holding you back isn't a lack of intelligence or opportunity, it's most likely fear. Fear of failing. Fear of getting it wrong. Fear of even looking at the truth.

One of the biggest fears my clients have is simply opening the envelopes or, in today's world, the portals, and facing the numbers and writing things down. Many of us dream without documenting. We have ideas, goals, and hopes swirling around in our minds, but they never make it onto paper. The moment you begin putting things down, they become real, and that can feel scary. What if the truth is worse than you thought? What if you start and don't follow through? I've been there too. But the secret is making your plan *wide enough*, with enough grace and flexibility built in, so you can stay within the guardrails and keep going.

Another fear I hear all the time is being the odd one out. The friend who actually has a financial plan. The woman who talks about investing or building wealth when everyone else is gossiping about vacation plans. It can feel lonely to be the one who wants more and who's brave enough to admit it. Many women still feel like it's selfish to want more—to build wealth, to pursue legacy wealth, to dream beyond "enough." But that's an old story. You can be generous *and* ambitious.

All of these fears often lead to avoidance. You might set your finances on autopilot, coasting along with whatever plan was put in place years ago without ever revisiting whether it still aligns with your life today. Sometimes, that autopilot was installed by someone else: a parent, a partner, a financial "expert" who meant well but didn't take the time to understand your values or your dreams.

Other times, it's simply the belief that money is too complicated to figure out. That you don't have the time, the knowledge, or the staying power to follow through. Maybe you've tried before and felt like you failed. We live in a world that constantly tells us what success should look like. Perfect homes. Perfect holidays. Perfect lunch boxes. If you're not doing it all flawlessly, you feel like you're falling behind. This is the opposite of abundance. It's exhaustion dressed up as achievement.

It's not your fault that all of this feels new. When you think about it, women have only really had financial independence at scale for roughly fifty years. That's not a long time. There are still very few visible role models for women who have built wealth and are willing to talk openly about it.

That lack of conversation creates isolation. It makes many women feel like they're the only ones who want more, or that wanting more is somehow selfish. But you're not alone. There's a quiet community of women just like you: wealth builders, dreamers, changemakers, who are doing this work, too.

When it comes to money, the biggest enemy isn't out there somewhere. It's often within. For many of us, the enemy is our past self who made decisions without enough information, or who absorbed unhelpful family beliefs like "money doesn't grow on trees" or "women shouldn't earn more than their husbands." These old scripts get embedded in our mindset and shape how we see ourselves and what we think we deserve.

Other enemies are more external, such as predatory lenders, credit card companies, and advertisers who profit from keeping us in a cycle of spending, stress, and self-doubt. They whisper, *"Buy now, pay later,"* and *"You deserve this,"* while pulling us further from financial freedom.

Your past doesn't define your future. You can rewrite your money story, reclaim your power, and create a different path for yourself and for generations to come.

Part of what keeps women feeling stuck is the constant barrage of marketing telling us that more products, more services, and more "conveniences" will make our lives better. In reality, it just makes our lives more complicated, and often, more expensive.

To feel truly rich and radiant, you have to unwind some of that noise. You have to get clear on what *you* really value, what *you* desire, and where your money can align with both. That sometimes means touching the flame of old money stories or fears, especially in relationships. Many women worry that taking charge financially will create tension with their partner or add one more item to their already long list of responsibilities. Ignoring it won't make it go away, but awareness will.

Mindfulness is simply awareness, and awareness is the first step to change. There's a belief that mindfulness and money don't mix. That being mindful is too "woo-woo," or that meditation belongs in yoga studios, not financial conversations. I'm here to tell you that you can meditate on your finances. You can visualize earning more, investing more, and giving more. You can connect with your money in a way that feels intentional and empowering, not stressful or shame-filled.

If you've ever found yourself staring at your bank account, scrolling through Instagram, or lying awake at night wondering if you're "doing it right," every woman I work with comes in carrying the same handful of questions, sometimes whispered, sometimes blurted out through a nervous laugh, but always from a place of wanting something more.

You might be wondering the same things:

- *Will this even work in today's economy?*
  With everything changing so quickly, it's easy to feel like the rules of money have shifted and that maybe you missed your chance.

- *What do I have to give up to feel secure finally?*
  So many financial programs focus on restriction—on what you *can't* have—rather than showing you what's possible when you start thinking in terms of *abundance* instead of *scarcity.*

- *How long will this take?*
  You want to know how much time and effort it will take to get out of debt, build wealth, and finally feel free. But the real shift begins the moment you begin.

- *How is this different from all the other programs that didn't work?*
  You've tried plans that felt rigid, disconnected, or out of touch with your values. You're looking for a relationship with your money that actually feels good rather than another set of rules.

- *How do I get my partner, friends, or family on board?*
  It's hard to make lasting changes in isolation. You want to know how to bring others along without feeling like you have to justify or shrink your dreams.

- *And finally, is it even possible for someone like me?*
  You might live in a high-cost area or work in a field where financial freedom seems impossible. You're wondering if *this* can really work for you.

This book is your invitation to stop asking *if* it's possible and start asking *how* it will look for you. Because the moment you believe that your version of wealth and radiance is within reach, you're already halfway there.

I didn't start this work because everything in my life was perfect. I started it because I hit a point where, from the outside, everything *looked* successful—my income, my achievements, my lifestyle—but inside, I felt disconnected. I had built what most people would call a highly successful life, yet it wasn't one I truly loved. That realization changed everything.

I began learning, unlearning, and relearning what it meant to have a healthy, thriving relationship with money. I moved through the stages of financial literacy, financial wellness, and finally, financial freedom, each one unlocking something deeper than just numbers on a spreadsheet. And what I've learned is that those stages are not permanent destinations. Sometimes you'll take two steps forward, one step back. Old thoughts and habits will pop up again. But each time they do, you'll know how to turn down their volume and return to the path with more wisdom, more peace, and more confidence than before.

I've coached hundreds of high-performing, driven, ambitious women who also crave calm, clarity, and harmony. And I teach them that stepping into abundance doesn't mean leaving ambition behind. I bring a unique blend of experience and training to this work. I'm a financial coach, a life coach, and a yoga and meditation teacher. This trifecta allows me to approach money from both a practical and a deeply human perspective, so you can align your money with your mind, body, and spirit to live fully and intentionally.

Today, I live what I teach. I've quadrupled my own financial freedom number, and now my money works for me, giving me the freedom to do meaningful work, travel, rest, and give generously. I'm no longer chasing "more" just for the sake of it. I'm curating a life that feels rich in every sense of the word.

My clients like to call me their *money mentor*, their *money mom*, or, as one of my favorites put it, their *rich and radiant cousin.* That's exactly how I see myself in this journey. I'm not here to lecture you from across the table. I'm here to sit beside you to help untangle the fear, rewrite your money story, and create a life that reflects the woman you are becoming.

When you truly engage with your money with intention, awareness, and self-compassion, everything begins to change. You feel calmer, more confident, and more in control, financially *and* emotionally. You begin to live *rich and radiant* right now, in the middle of your journey, not someday when your bank account finally "proves it."

That silent questioning—*Am I doing this right? Will I ever get there?*—starts to fade. You'll have a map, a way to track your progress, and the reassurance that you're on the path. You'll build a safety net that gives you the courage to take risks, earn more, and make bold moves without fear of losing yourself along the way.

And when you do, you'll begin creating legacy wealth that supports your life and uplifts others. When women have financial freedom, they change families, communities, and the world. Mindful money ripples outward into every part of life; your relationships, your health, your happiness. You just feel better. You think clearly. You turn down the volume on the negative self-talk that's been running the show for far too long.

Most of all, you'll realize you're not alone. I want this book to feel like sitting beside a friend who gets it, someone who's been where you are and walked this same path. Let it be your guide, your sounding board, your quiet conversation partner as you sort through your facts and your feelings. Read it on your own or start a book club with your girlfriends. Have the conversations that matter, the ones that help us rise together.

I wrote *Rich and Radiant* because years ago, sitting in a little sushi restaurant with my husband, I wrote "write a book" on the bucket list we had created on the paper tablecloth. I didn't know it then, but that small promise to myself would turn into this: a love letter to every woman who's ever felt capable yet uncertain, accomplished yet unfulfilled, successful yet disconnected from her own wealth.

I've done the rewiring, the relearning, the rebuilding. I've lived the gap between "fine" and *fulfilled*. So come sit next to me. You don't have to have it all figured out. You just have to start.

- Liz Carroll

PART ONE

Survive

Educate with Empathy

CHAPTER ONE

From Avoidance to Awareness

Think of this chapter as your invitation. This is the moment where you stop chasing more information, more podcasts, more articles, more frantic Googling, and you finally begin building wealth from a grounded, safe place in the present. Because so often, you think about money in the past, the mistakes, the regrets, the "I should have done it differently." Or you're living in the future, the what-ifs, the unknowns, the fears of what might come.

But real change only happens in the present. Mindfulness brings you right here, into the now. And there is no better time than this moment to start your wealth-building journey.

Now, some of what you've been carrying around may not belong on this trip. You might have old thoughts or emotions around money that feel heavy, unhelpful, or outdated. Beliefs about what you're allowed to earn, what you're capable of managing, or whether you "deserve" to invest and grow wealth. You may even have inherited ideas about who benefits from money, and whether you're supposed to be one of those people.

This chapter helps you prepare emotionally, mentally, and practically so you can travel light. Remember that this is entirely about you — your values, your dreams, your relationship with money, your vision of a rich and radiant life.

Where Avoidance Really Comes From

The real reason high-earning, high-achieving women avoid looking at their numbers has nothing to do with being "too busy." That's just the surface-level excuse. It sounds acceptable in conversation, but doesn't match what's happening underneath.

What's really going on is this: You were never taught.

Not really. Not in a way that reflects your reality as a modern woman with access, autonomy, income, and opportunity that previous generations did not have. For centuries, women passed down recipes, relationship wisdom, and household skills, but no one passed down financial confidence. Our grandmothers never had the experience with money that you do now. Even our mothers didn't have access to the investment tools, retirement accounts, income potential, or the independence you have today. Much of what modern women can do with money has only existed for the last 50 years.

So, of course, you feel uncertain. Of course, money feels triggering. How could you magically "just know" what to do?

When you feel unsure, you freeze. When you're scared you'll mess something up, you avoid it. When you remember a single mistake from years ago, the one moment you lost money or felt irresponsible, you pull that old feeling into the present and assume it still defines you.

And part of your work now is to ask: Is that belief true for me today? Or am I carrying a ghost from the past?

In my coaching practice, I've learned that most women are dealing with the fear of opening the portal: Logins they never click, accounts they haven't checked in years, balances they're afraid to look at because they're convinced something scary is waiting for them on the other side.

But what they usually find is that the scariest part was the not knowing. When I sit down with clients and we open their accounts together, they often realize they are doing so much better than they had ever allowed themselves to believe.

Even a simple move, like shifting money from a standard savings account earning almost nothing to a high-yield savings account, can give you the momentum and confidence to make the next intentional money move. This kind of confidence can open the doors to investing. Avoidance dissolves the moment empowerment begins. Confidence comes from trying. From being willing to make a few mistakes, learn from them, and course correct.

I've made money mistakes. We all have. And it's okay.

The Pressure of "Should"

Your brain loves to focus on danger. It exaggerates the negative and hides the positive. Without training, it constantly whispers the same old message: *You've messed this up. You're behind. You should know more by now.* Many of my clients have advanced degrees. They are doctors, lawyers, executives, entrepreneurs; brilliant, capable women. And yet, they still have hang-ups around money because they believe that being smart in one area means they "should" automatically be good at finances too.

But intelligence in one domain doesn't automatically translate to another. If you were never shown a path, how would you know which steps to take?

That pressure — that word *should* — can be incredibly damaging. "Should" feels like shame to me. And when I feel ashamed, I withdraw.

Many women struggle to celebrate their financial wins, even with other women, because they worry about what their success means. They've been "shoulded on" their whole lives about what kind of career they should have, what kind of mother they should be, what kind of money choices they should make.

And now they're being "shoulded on" about how they should spend, save, or dream with their money. The message is often: don't be ambitious, don't aim too high, don't shine too brightly. Just save quietly and stay grateful.

The Unspoken Fears Successful Women Carry

Underneath avoidance sits something deeper. Even the most competent, educated, successful women carry quiet fears about money, shaped by the stories they've been told about financially successful women.

Think of the cultural examples we've grown up with. When a woman is powerful in the movies, she's often portrayed as lonely or unapproachable. Miranda Priestly in *The Devil Wears Prada* — brilliant, yes, but isolated, surrounded by people who want something from her.

And look at older films: the wealthy woman wasn't the respected business owner; she owned the brothel. She was stigmatized rather than celebrated. These stories whisper that money will isolate us. That success will cost us connection. That wanting more makes us less "good."

Even in real life, we haven't had many positive female money mentors. Many spiritual figures we admire took vows of poverty, reinforcing the idea that "good women" give everything away. In most families, money conversations were avoided or rooted in fear. In most corporations, financially empowered women were rare enough to feel like exceptions. Money naturally feels complicated when you're trying to build something you've rarely seen modeled.

The Subtle Signs of Financial Autopilot

Amongst all of this avoidance and fear, you might not even realize you're on financial autopilot. From the outside, everything looks "fine." You're functioning. You're paying your bills. You're contributing to retirement. You're doing the responsible things.

But inside your day-to-day life, autopilot shows up in quiet, draining ways.

1. You Do the Bare Minimum

This might look like making the minimum payment on a student loan or credit card simply because that's the number someone else decided. It might look like following the advice from people who don't know your values, dreams, or desires.

2. You Don't Track or Plan — You Just Hope

You spend without clarity and then hope it all works out. Meanwhile, in the back of your mind, a little voice keeps asking:*"Is this okay? Am I doing this right?"*

That quiet questioning becomes exhausting. It drains your energy more than looking at the numbers ever would.

3. You Contribute to Retirement... But Don't Understand It

You're putting money in, but you don't really know:

- If the amount is right
- If the options match your goals
- If you're over-contributing or under-contributing
- How your debt impacts those decisions

You're checking the box, but the box doesn't feel meaningful.

4. You're Living in Past Decisions

Old debt keeps you anchored to old choices. You're making payments for something that no longer exists in your life, which keeps your emotional relationship with money stuck in the past, too.

Imagine how different you'd feel if you were fully in the *present* with your money.

5. You Keep Putting It Off

"I'll get to it later."
"I'll look at it this weekend."
"Once a year is enough."

The contradiction is that money is the number one cause of stress in women's lives, and yet it sits at the bottom of the list. How can the thing causing the most stress be the thing you're "too busy" to deal with?

You're avoiding it because you think it will take up tons of your time or be too much to handle. Some companies and institutions benefit financially from making wealth-building seem complex, intimidating, or inaccessible. They profit when you feel overwhelmed.

But here's what I want every woman to understand:

True wealth-building doesn't require anything more than fifth-grade math.
And you passed fifth grade.

Once you get organized with routines, systems, and rhythms, it takes very little time at all. What it really requires is intention.

The Power of the Pause

When it comes to money, the "power of the pause" is one of the most important tools you have, and it's also the simplest. You'll know you need the pause if you're reading this book. If you felt called to open these pages, you already know something in your financial life needs a moment of presence.

The pause is your chance to prepare yourself before you take a financial action or, in many cases, before you stay in inaction. It's a brief moment where you name the emotion, the energy, or the story sitting underneath whatever you're doing (or not doing) with your money.

Why aren't you moving forward on your financial wellness or financial freedom journey?

Why does money feel hard?

These questions only take a couple of seconds to ask, but they bring you into clarity. When you pause, breathe, and feel what's actually going on inside you, you get to step out of autopilot and into awareness. And awareness is what opens the door to healing, intention, and real change.

Sometimes the pause is as simple as asking yourself:

"When it comes to money, what am I afraid of?"

That one moment of honesty can shift everything.

How Awareness Begins

When I help a woman begin shifting into awareness, I don't start with spreadsheets or budgets. I don't start with numbers at all. I start with that pause where you breathe, feel, and turn inward toward your own heart center.

The first question I ask is:

What are your unique values?

Not the values you think you "should" have. Not the ones you inherited. Not the ones your career or your family has placed on you. *Yours.*

I often ask women to identify their top five values, which can be anything from beauty, personal growth, and creativity to faith, wellness, adventure, rest, or connection. Once you've anchored into your values, we take the next step — and this one can feel surprisingly challenging:

What are your desires?

I ask for twenty-five desires — things, feelings, or experiences you want to bring into your life. And yes, most women struggle with this at first. They'll often list things they already possess, because desiring something new feels uncomfortable or unfamiliar. When that happens, I remind them: it's okay to include a few things you appreciate, but I'm also asking for *new* desires. I'm asking for expansion.

When you know what matters most (your values) and you know what you want (your desires), we can begin aligning your money with both. This is the part that creates the biggest transformation. You'll start asking:

How can my money support the dreams I have for my life?

How can it help me create the experiences, safety, impact, and fulfillment I desire?

When your money finally has a purpose that's connected to *you*, not what someone else says you should want, everything becomes more intentional.

There's a moment I see in almost every woman I work with when I know she has moved out of avoidance and into awareness. It's subtle, but powerful.

She exhales. It's a deep, honest, grounded exhale that comes from finally feeling supported, finally having a plan, and finally realizing she doesn't have to do this alone. That exhale is her whole nervous system saying, *"Oh… I'm safe now."*

This is what awareness looks like at the beginning:

She gives herself space and grace. She allows herself to learn without judgment. She understands that being scared makes sense because no one taught her these things yet. She begins to trust that she knows more than she has given herself credit for.

And then the biggest shift happens:

She stops overthinking and starts taking mindful action. The circular thoughts that kept her stuck in inaction start to quiet down. She no longer spins in fear about what she "should" know or what she "might" mess up. Instead, she takes small, intentional steps with calm confidence.

Your First Step Forward

As we close this chapter, I want to bring you back to the heart of everything we've said: pause for awareness. Pause long enough to reconnect with your values. No one else gets to define what matters most in your life, and no one else gets to decide what your money should support.

Your values, your desires, and your financial facts are the foundation for building wealth. When you know what you value, when you know what you truly want, and when you know your numbers, you suddenly have truth instead of stories.

So start with the simple stuff:

What do you own?
What do you owe?
What is your net worth today?

You know more than you think you do, and you're doing better than you think you are. Most women discover this the moment they finally open the portals, look at their accounts, and see the facts. A few small tweaks, some straightforward systems, and intentional organization can change how your money works for you and how you feel about your entire financial life.

Your money can support the desires and outcomes you dream about. But it starts with safety, mindfulness, and a moment of presence to assess your situation honestly and gently.

And then the most important part is choosing the next best money move for you. Not the perfect one. Not the one someone says you "should" do.

Trust yourself.

Trust that you can learn, grow, and lead your money instead of fearing it.

KEY TAKEAWAYS

- Avoidance is the natural result of never being taught how to navigate money in a way that reflects your life, your power, and your reality today.
- The fear lives in the unknown, not the numbers; clarity dissolves anxiety the moment you open the portals and see the truth.
- "Should" creates shame, and shame shuts you down. Awareness begins when you pause, breathe, and ask what's really driving your hesitation.
- Your values and desires are the compass. When your money aligns with what matters most to you, intention replaces autopilot.
- Small, mindful steps build confidence. You don't need perfection, just the courage to pause, look honestly, and choose your next best move.

CHAPTER TWO

Math of the Moment: Facing the Numbers

You need to know the facts of your situation. This chapter is about working with what *is*, not what you fear, imagine, or hope your numbers might be someday. When you work with facts, you give yourself the gift of clarity. And the beautiful thing I see again and again is that the facts are often *better* than the fictional version you're carrying around in your mind.

Awareness is part of mindfulness, and that's why the previous chapter focused so much on building awareness. Now we're going deeper by looking at the actual numbers. And let me say this clearly: Your net worth is not your self-worth. Those two things must be separated. Net worth is a data point. It's one of the measures we use to understand your financial picture. Income and wealth are not the same thing, and for high-achieving women, especially, it is essential to distinguish between them.

I've worked with many women who earn incredible income yet haven't built wealth, not because they're incapable, but because no one ever taught them the link between income and investing for their future selves.

A significant misunderstanding that many successful women carry is equating high income with financial success. Income is what's visible. It's what people talk about. It's posted on LinkedIn, whispered about over brunch, and built into the status structure of careers. But income is not wealth. And we do not talk about that difference nearly enough. You can have a very high income and still not build wealth. I see it all the time. The moment we start observing the actual flow of money rather than the image of income, we often notice:

- More money is flowing *out* than flowing *in*, or
- Very little is being directed toward the results they truly desire.

That's where values come in. When you align your numbers with your values, everything shifts. I encourage my clients to define what success means to *them,* not to their industry, their peers, or the algorithm.

When you access your heart center, success rarely revolves around money. It's about feelings, connections, time, experiences, freedom, and peace. Money is simply the bridge that allows those feelings and experiences to flourish. It creates options and opportunities. But it is rarely the end goal itself.

Documenting Your Numbers vs. Dreaming Your Numbers

I've worked with many women who dream their numbers instead of documenting them. And dreaming can be dangerous because it distorts reality, creates pressure, and leads to fear-driven decisions.

I once worked with a client who had an annual compensation package of $500,000. That was the number she held in her mind. She walked around thinking, I make half a million dollars a year. And technically, yes... but not all of that ever touched her checking account or was available for spending.

She had deferred compensation. She had taxes. She had benefit deductions. She had retirement contributions. So living as though she had $500,000 of spendable money created stress, chaos, and eventually what she described as "financial nightmares." Life didn't match the fantasy number she kept referencing.

This is why documenting your take-home income, your real, actual, factual inflow, is so important. That is the number we plan from.

When you document, two things happen:

- You stop making plans based on fiction.
- You finally hear what you actually want.

This part is magical. When women slow down enough to document their reality, they begin to access desires that come from their hearts and souls rather than from comparison. When clients settle into themselves, what rises isn't loud. It's not flashy. It's not the performative "should" goals or the socially conditioned numbers that have been chasing you around for years.

And physically writing it down reveals it. Pen to paper helps bring forward the desires you didn't even know you had; the ones that actually belong to you.

Calculating Your Net Worth and Cash Flow Gently

When we calculate your net worth or cash flow, the very first thing we anchor into is mindfulness. This means observing *without judgment*. We're not labeling anything as good or bad. We're not attaching morality or worthiness to the numbers. We're only looking at facts.

Your net worth is just that—a data point. It doesn't reflect your identity, value, and it certainly isn't the final verdict on your past choices.

It is simply:
What you own (your assets)
minus
What you owe (your liabilities)

Sometimes gathering those numbers feels like a little scavenger hunt. You're opening accounts, pulling statements, and finding logins you haven't used in a while. But I always provide an easy spreadsheet that does the math for you. And I want you to know this, because it happens nine out of ten times: once it's all entered, women say, *"I'm actually doing better than I thought."* And the emotional response is pure relief.

For so long, you've been dreading this moment. You've avoided looking at the numbers because you assume they'll confirm a fear or expose something you don't want to see. But when you look directly at the truth, the dread dissolves. You feel grounded again.

From relief comes the next feeling: Hope. Facts create plans, and plans create hope. Suddenly, the disorganization, chaos, and shame that once felt overwhelming begin to settle. You move from *"I don't want to look at this"* to *"Okay, I see what's happening. Now what can we do?"*

And here's the part that still gives me goosebumps: most women realize they can absolutely reach their desired outcome. The numbers show a pathway. They can see it. They can feel it. Sometimes they just need someone sitting next to them while they take that first courageous look. Someone they can borrow confidence from until their own confidence grows strong enough to stand on its own.

As a coach, I often have more confidence in my clients than they have in themselves. I feel a bit like a kindergarten teacher, gently encouraging, saying, *"I know you can do this."* Because so much of the fear around money is old wiring messages like, *"I'm not good at math," "This is too confusing,"* or *"I always mess this up."* Together, we rewrite that script.

Observing the Ocean

Cash flow becomes gentler when you stop treating it like a performance review and start treating it like watching the tides. I always reference the ocean and the way waves move in and out with such calm inevitability. When you observe your cash flow like that, you take yourself out of the equation and become the observer. You watch the flow of "the" money, not the flow of "my" money.

You look at:

- How it comes in
- How much goes out
- Whether you like where it's going
- Whether something wants to shift

Through that calm observing, you start to see what you want to change and what already feels aligned.

The "Fingers Closed" Visualization

There's a visualization I love that resonates deeply with so many women. Imagine holding your hands out to receive money, open, welcoming, and ready. But then imagine that instead of keeping your fingers gently closed, you spread them wide open. What happens? The money slips right through.

I often see women receiving large sums but not holding on long enough to engage with them, decide what they truly want to do with them, or put them to work for their future selves.

Closing your fingers not in a tight, fearful grip, but in a mindful, intentional way, symbolizes staying present with your money rather than letting it flow out faster than it flows in.

The ability to hold onto money is a terrific skill to practice, especially if you think, *"If I have it, I'll spend it."*

Dealing with Debt

Debt carries so much shame. It's often a secret; no one knows your number by looking at you. People may guess your weight, but they cannot guess your debt. So it gets tucked away, hidden, creating emotional weight.

I like to encourage women to gamify their debt payoff. When debt becomes a game, it becomes energizing. I teach three debt payoff strategies:

- The Snowball: Momentum-focused. Sequence debt payoff from the smallest debt balance to the largest debt balance.

- The Avalanche: Math-focused. Sequence debt payoff from the highest interest rate first, then work your way to the lowest interest rate.
- The Annoyance: Energy-focused. Which debt bothers you the most (maybe tax penalties, attorney fees, or a parental loan)? Start there and get that debt out of your life first.

Each strategy has benefits. But the *real* benefit is building a sequence that you actually follow. Because taking action is what changes your life, not just choosing a method.

As a yoga teacher, I think about this as creating a sequence of poses. I choose the order based on the experience I want my students to have in class. Debt payoff is the same. We pause, breathe, feel... and then create a sequence that feels good and motivating for *you*.

The part most women don't realize is that you don't have to pick just one strategy. I have clients who start with the annoyance, switch to the avalanche to eliminate the highest interest rate, and then move into the snowball for the rest. Or, the snowball to gain momentum, then switch to the avalanche. You get to build your own sequence.

Debt Is the Past—How Long Do You Want to Stay There?

Debt often feels heavy because debt is the past. It's the echo of decisions you once made.

So I ask women questions like:

- How long do you want to stay in the past?
- Do you have a date in mind for when you want to be done carrying this?
- What will it feel like to make decisions in the present again?

And then I invite their future self into the conversation. She gets a vote too.

What does she want for you?
How long does she want you to stay in the past?
What pace feels right for her?

When you shift into the present and start making money decisions for today and for her, everything changes. Living debt-free means every dollar that comes in can now be directed intentionally. You decide its purpose. And yes, some debts are intentional and even desired. That's perfectly okay. What matters is knowing where they belong in your sequence.

Playing the "What If?" Game from Hope and Creativity

Gamifying debt also means creating possibilities. One of my favorite tools is the *What If?* Game.

- What if you generated an additional $1,000 per month for debt payoff?
- How would that change the math?
- How would it move up your debt-free date?

- What could you do to generate that extra income?
- How could you make it playful?
- What would your debt payoff timeline look like with that extra energy behind it?

When you bring curiosity rather than shame, debt payoff becomes a hopeful (and even fun) creative process. Play with the numbers and timeline, then settle into a plan that feels motivating and encouraging.

Creating Rituals That Make Tracking Your Numbers Feel Sacred

I absolutely love tracking my cash flow. I track it daily on an app on my phone because that rhythm works beautifully for me. But that doesn't mean it's the right approach for everyone. With clients, we experiment. We try different tools, different rhythms, different ways of engaging until we find what feels supportive. Tracking is ultimately about awareness, and awareness is a mindful practice. It takes repetition, trial and error, and patience. And it evolves into a habit, then a routine, then a ritual.

I like to think of tracking as a *sacred ritual* that keeps me safe on the wealth-building path I've chosen. That language—*I have chosen this path*—keeps me rooted in agency. I know where I'm headed, and I like where I'm going. Because of that, the ritual doesn't feel burdensome. It feels aligned, like meditation or breathwork.

For me, daily tracking works much like a dental or skincare routine. I've seen real success with that level of consistency. But your ritual might be weekly. It might be monthly. It only needs to fit *you.*

The important part is that it becomes a rhythm in your life, not a once-a-year panic session where everything feels urgent, overwhelming, and too late. When tracking is a ritual, it is grounding.

One of the most powerful things that happens when you document your numbers is that your spending suddenly comes into focus. You start asking different questions:

- Is this aligned with where I want my money to go?
- Is this supporting my desired wealth-building path?
- Is this spending bringing me joy or convenience, or is it a habit?
- Do I need any course corrections?

I see food spending come up often. Not because food itself is the issue, but because convenience food—eating out, delivery apps, services—can quietly stack up without you realizing it. And once women see the real number, they often say, *"I had no idea I was spending that much… and half of it I don't even enjoy."*

Documenting shifts the entire relationship with spending from autopilot to intention. Sometimes the answer is, *Yes, this is absolutely worth it.* And other times, it's, *No, this isn't aligned with my values anymore.*

From there, you naturally begin defining categories and guardrails. You decide how much you *want* to spend in certain areas, rather than waking up shocked by what has already happened. This is where new freedom emerges:

- The freedom to choose more aligned spending.
- The freedom to redirect money toward your true desires.
- The freedom to shape a financial life you *actually want*.

Letting Go of Shame and Finding Freedom

I want to share a story about a woman who dreaded what she called "budgeting." And first, let me say this: I don't like to use the B-word. Words create feelings, and budgeting often feels restrictive, punitive, or guilt-laden. So I always call it a *plan*, a cash flow plan, or a spending plan.

This client of mine was highly educated, from prestigious schools, and incredibly smart. And yet she carried so much guilt, shame, and resentment around her money story. It was the last area of her life she hadn't touched, even though she had done so much personal growth work everywhere else.

When we finally sat down together and faced it, yes, there were tears. There was an unwinding of beliefs. There was understanding and compassion for the resentment and guilt she had carried. Her feelings made perfect sense once we explored their origins, particularly the beliefs she had inherited from her immigrant parents.

But then something beautiful happened.

Once she created her spending plan and she could visually see where her money was going and compare that to where she *wanted* it to go, making changes suddenly felt easy and freeing, even. The relief she felt was almost immediate. She stepped into a more modern relationship with money that matched the life she was actually living and the income she was actually earning.

A year later, after becoming a mother and navigating major life changes, she wrote to me. She told me she felt powerful. She said she had continued working her plan every single month, and it helped her bring more of what she truly desired into her life.

Before we met, she believed that she wasn't good with money. That she couldn't understand it. It surprised her that it was easier than she feared, and that she could stick with it for a whole year during one of the most chaotic seasons of her life. She now felt a sense of freedom and calm from creating a monthly practice. This transformation occurs when you stop dreaming your numbers and start documenting them with compassion.

Step Into the Math of the Moment

Befriend the factual numbers. They are always less scary than the fictional ones in your head. This chapter is your invitation to become an observer, a watcher, not a judge. Witness the flow of money with the same calm neutrality a birdwatcher brings to the forest. Just noticing, documenting, and seeing what is true.

From that truth, you can redirect your money toward outcomes that align with your values and desires and replace anxiety with intention.Make tracking your numbers a ritual, a routine, a sacred practice just like brushing your teeth, caring for your skin, or moving your body. You get to decide what rhythm works best for you: daily, weekly, or monthly. Consistency matters more than frequency.

And remember that wealth is built by putting a portion of your income to work.

I love thinking of it as *my money's money*. My money's money is working for me every single day. In the United States, the average millionaire has eight streams of income from side hustles, rental properties, owning part of a business, investment income, or stock portfolios. Many of those are the result of decisions made years ago to put money aside for their future self.

You can do the same. You are fully capable. And the moment you can observe your numbers with curiosity instead of fear, everything changes. This is the math of the moment.

KEY TAKEAWAYS

- Your numbers are never a verdict on your worth. They're simply facts, and facing them with compassion brings clarity, relief, and hope.
- Documenting your cash flow reveals what you actually want, dissolves fear-based decisions, and grounds you in desires that come from your heart rather than comparison.
- Observing your money like the ocean, calmly, without judgment, helps you see where it flows, what feels aligned, and what wants to shift.
- Debt is the past; when you gamify it, sequence it, and invite your future self into the process, you transform shame into empowerment and momentum.
- Turning tracking into a ritual connects you to your money with intention, helping you redirect it toward freedom, aligned choices, and the life you truly want.

CHAPTER THREE

Building Safety Nets

Many women I work with are walking a financial tightrope, sometimes literally, but more often in their minds. Picture it: a tightrope stretched across a canyon. When you're standing there, frozen, all you're focused on is not falling. You're not moving forward. You're not looking ahead. You're not building momentum. You're just trying to survive. Living in this constant survival mode takes a real toll, both emotionally and financially. It's a hidden cost: hours lost to worry, sleepless nights, and missed chances to grow or invest because of fear. If you added up that cost over a year, it would be surprising. That's why stepping off this mental tightrope can change everything.

Financial fear paralyzes you. And when you're paralyzed, you don't take mindful action to build wealth. You might be getting by, but feeling wealthy and getting by are two very different things. One is survival. The other is stability, choice, and calm confidence.

Feeling financially secure makes it easier to move forward, grow, earn more, and take on more responsibility. But when fear is in control, you miss out on opportunities because all your energy goes into just staying afloat.

Safety Is Not Just a Number

A common question is: What comes first? Does having money in your account make you feel safe, or does having the right mindset help you feel secure enough to move ahead?

I don't believe it's one or the other. I think it's both.

Mindset and numbers work together. When you start to feel more confident and have a clear path, you can begin taking steps forward. As you move forward, you build the safety net that strengthens your confidence.

Language matters here. You'll notice I don't call this an "emergency fund." I don't know about you, but I have never felt calm or grounded calling 911. That word alone puts your nervous system on edge. Words create sensations in the body. And when your body is living in a constant state of fight, flight, fawn, or freeze, it's almost impossible to move forward financially. What I see most often with my clients isn't fight-or-flight. It's freeze. They're not doing anything. They're avoiding decisions. They're stuck, not because they're incapable, but because their nervous system doesn't feel safe.

It's not a coincidence that when I started meditating more, I made more money. When I cleaned up my debt, I made more money. When my safety net was built, I made more money. A safety net allows us to take risks. It is there to support us if we fall. It doesn't assume disaster. It assumes growth.

The Financial Relief Plan

When I talk about a financial relief plan, what I really mean is this: building a financial safety net is often the first goal that creates forward movement. It brings relief from the constant worry and anxiety about making the "wrong" financial decision.

We start with the facts. We look at your cash flow so you can clearly see what's coming in, what's going out, and what's possible. When you understand your numbers, you stop guessing and start making confident decisions.

From there, we define what "financial safety" actually means for you. This is personal. For some, it's a certain amount in savings. For others, it's knowing their bills are covered for a set period of time. What matters is that you feel a sense of stability and control.

When those two pieces come together, something powerful happens. You begin to feel relief. Instead of worrying that one misstep could derail everything, you see that you have options. Your financial relief plan serves as a guide, showing you where you're going and reminding you that there are multiple ways to get there. You get to choose the path that aligns with your life, your values, and your vision.

Your Financial Independence Number

Your financial independence number, your FI number, is the vision for your future self. It represents a place where work becomes optional. Not because you stop caring or lose ambition, but because you have a choice. Financial freedom is when your assets (or your money's money) generate enough income to cover your expenses.

Getting there often requires your present self to clean up some of the decisions your past self made, especially when it comes to debt. I like to think of this as a continuum. There's the past, where debt may exist. There's the present, where you're creating safety. And there's the future, where financial independence lives. Your FI number is the destination. It's a form of distance and measurement indicating where you are headed.

To calculate your financial independence (FI) number, multiply your desired annual expenses by 25 (based on the 4% rule). For example, if you need $80,000 annually, your FI number is $2 million ($80,000 x 25). You would need a $2M investment portfolio to cover expenses without working by withdrawing 4% or $80,000 annually. However, real estate investing is a little different and doesn't follow the 4% rule like a stock market investment portfolio. As a real estate investor, you would need a property portfolio netting at least $6,500 per month in cash flow to generate $80,000 of income.

And I want to be very clear about something: knowing or attaining your FI number does not mean you'll stop working or set your ambition aside. It's purely a number. It shows you where you'll have the opportunity to make work optional.

I didn't stop working when I hit my FI number. In fact, I doubled it before leaving my W-2 job. What it gave me was freedom and flexibility. My energy shifted.

When I built a safety net, I went from scared to feeling safe. From safety, I was able to grow successfully. That's the journey. Knowing where you've been, where you are now, and where you're going allows you to make grounded decisions in the present for your future self.

Debt Is Not a Moral Failing

Many high-achieving women equate debt with failure. When that belief shows up, the first thing I ask is:

How does that feel?
How is that helpful for you?
Where does feeling like a failure actually get you?

It's not motivating to pay down debt when you're beating yourself up. Shame does not create momentum. Remember that debt is merely a circumstance and a solvable problem. Instead of seeing debt as a failure, try asking, 'What lesson is this debt teaching me about future wealth?' This reframing shifts the narrative from shame to growth and possibility.

I choose to live debt-free now because I like being in the present, but that wasn't always the case. There were times when I took on debt to buy assets, like real estate. I viewed that as strategic debt, and I entered those agreements with a very clear repayment plan, one that my future self was happy with.

Where I see challenges arise is with debt that has no clear repayment strategy or debt tied to non-appreciating items. That's when it starts to weigh on your energy.

So we pause and ask:

How heavy does this feel?
How is it holding you back in your financial wellness journey?
Is this helping you move toward freedom, or away from it?

Debt is figure-outable. I often encourage clients to create a repayment plan where the debt is paid off within 24 months, especially for consumer debt, so they can return to living in the present sooner rather than later.

I have a client right now whose minimum payments have kept her stuck in credit card debt for over six years. We reworked the plan, and now she'll be done in 24 months. That shift alone changes how she shows up in her life.

Intentional Rewards vs. Lingering Regret

Now let's talk about non-appreciating purchases. I very much believe in rewarding yourself. In my sales career, I intentionally set aside 10% of my commissions for rewards. I did that on purpose. I was happy with my savings rate. I was pleased with my investment rate. The reward came from a grounded, intentional place.

If a purchase doesn't negatively impact your energy, it's not a problem. But if it sets you back financially, creates stress the next day, or buyer's remorse that creeps in immediately, that's usually a sign there's a money story worth cleaning up.

Here's the key question: Does the purchase decision create positive energy or negative energy?

Sometimes confidence does increase because of something tangible. And if that confidence helps you show up more fully, create more opportunity, or build more business, then that choice may be right for you.

I've had beautiful cars. Right now, I drive a Tahoe, not because it's flashy, but because I can fit three car seats across the backseat. And I love it. I feel rich and radiant because I get to put my three grandkids in that car.

That's what intentional wealth looks like. When your choices support your energy, your present, and your future, you're building a safety net that actually holds you.

The False Sense of Safety

One of the most common false safety nets I see is credit cards. Many women rely on them as their backup plan. But that's not a safety net. That's borrowing someone else's.

I encourage you to shift from depending on someone else to save you to becoming your own safety net. The same applies to home equity lines or lines of credit. I have both, but neither is my safety nor my safety net. They're tools, not protection.

Another pattern I see often is overbuying insurance, car insurance, homeowners insurance, even cell phone insurance, instead of intentionally self-insuring through a true safety net. A real safety net lets you bear some of the risks yourself. And when you can do that, it often reduces your monthly outflow of money and gives you more flexibility.

The false sense of safety comes from believing that someone else, a bank, a credit card, a lender, will rescue you if something goes wrong. Your best safety net is you.

From Scared to Safe

There's a moment I see again and again when a safety net starts to take shape. The self-doubt begins to evaporate. I'm thinking of one client in particular, though this has happened for many women I've worked with, and what changed first wasn't her bank account. It was her internal state.

As her safety net strengthened, her confidence blossomed. The anxiety that had been quietly running in the background began to fade. And almost immediately, new opportunities started to appear, career growth, investment opportunities, possibilities she couldn't see before.

It's as if once we move from scared to safe, we naturally step into success. There was a sense of peace that came over her. A grounded calm. And with that calm, she stopped spending so much energy worrying. That freed-up energy got redirected.

She grew her business to heights she never anticipated. At the same time, she began repairing her relationship with her mother. When the constant hum of financial anxiety quieted, she had the capacity to show up differently in her life.

When worry loosens its grip, self-doubt falls away. And in that space, confidence, clarity, and connection have room to grow. The magical thing about safety nets is that, yes, they support your finances, but they also support *you.*

Right-Sizing Your Safety Net and What Comes Next

Your safety net is a bit like Goldilocks. You don't want it too small, and you don't want it too big. It needs to be just right for you. That size will be unique to your individual cash flow plan, your career and your personal money story. When a safety net gets too large, you can actually start missing investment opportunities. Money that could be working for you sits in a high yield savings account instead of invested in higher earning opportunities. Three to six months of required monthly expenses is a good rule of thumb.

This is why it's so important to know your numbers and understand your internal sense of security. We'll work more on the emotional side of feeling safe later in the book, but once your safety net is right-sized, you'll know. There's a feeling of "enoughness" that settles in. And from there, you move into what I call your freedom fund.

I don't have two clients with the same safety net amount. And once that net is in place, the next step is intentional investing, putting your money to work for you in income-producing assets.

That might mean investing in yourself through education or skill-building. It could be mutual or index funds, a business, or real estate. Real estate is my favorite because it worked for me. I like that I can touch it, improve it, and be creative with it, unlike a share of stock, where I have no control and own the same piece as everyone else.

There are many paths to building wealth. What matters is finding the one that feels right for you.

My own safety net includes cash on hand, cash in a high-yield savings account, and some physical hard currency like gold and silver, for if things really hit the fan. I don't view any of it as an investment. I view it as insurance for me moving forward and having the freedom to invest in opportunities as they arise.

If you're just starting, think small and tangible. Enough to buy a cell phone outright. Enough to cover your insurance deductibles. Then build it to a set number of months of expenses and place it in a high-yield savings account so it's working for you, too. Label it something encouraging in your bank's online portal, a nickname like "I've got you" or "You're doing great."

I use the interest from mine each year for a girlfriend's getaway weekend. You could keep the interest building, use it for holiday spending, or do something fun that reminds you why you're doing this in the first place. There are so many creative ways to establish a feeling of safety as soon as possible.

As your financial confidence builds, your safety net may actually shrink. Not because you're reckless, but because you trust yourself more. You know things are figure-outable. You can see opportunities clearly. When you're sitting on the sidelines, frozen in fear, walking that mental tightrope, you miss everything on the other side. What opportunity will you finally see when fear loosens its grip? Imagine the possibilities that could unfold as your future self steps confidently into a new reality.

A true safety net saves you money, saves you worry, and most importantly, it preserves your energy. That preserved energy is what allows you to step forward, invest wisely, and live a life that feels rich and radiant.

KEY TAKEAWAYS

- Financial safety is created by both mindset and numbers working together; when your nervous system feels safe, you can take grounded action.
- A true safety net is not about preparing for disaster, but about supporting growth, choice, and the ability to take thoughtful risks.
- Debt is a circumstance, not a moral failing, and when it has a clear, intentional plan, it stops draining your energy and starts freeing your future.
- False safety comes from relying on credit, lenders, or insurance instead of becoming your own source of stability and self-trust.
- When your safety net is right-sized, fear loosens its grip, opportunities become visible, and you're finally positioned to move from safety into intentional wealth-building.

PART TWO

Strive

Excel with Ease

CHAPTER FOUR

The Voice of Fear vs. The Voice of Love

Earlier in this book, we talked about fear as something that keeps you avoidant. Fear can keep you from looking at your numbers, from walking the tightrope, and from taking the next honest step forward. But fear does not only show up as avoidance. For many high-earning, high-achieving women, it shows up as striving, as pushing, and as chasing external success. When was the last time fear nudged your decisions or actions? This gentle acknowledgment helps us recognize that you're not alone in this journey. Fear is a common thread that links us, and it often invites the ego to quietly step in and take the lead.

The voice of fear sometimes says, "Do more," "Try harder," or "Prove yourself again." It disguises itself as ambition and productivity, and because it looks so familiar, it often goes unquestioned. The voice of fear expresses itself through many behaviors, but most of us move too quickly to notice the energy behind them. We are responding, reacting, accomplishing, and checking things off without ever pausing to ask why. This chapter is an invitation to get quiet and to listen beneath the noise of your to-do list.

When Ego Shows Up in Money Decisions

Ego energy often shows up in money decisions through comparison and quiet resentment. It sounds like, "I should be further ahead," without ever stopping to ask, further ahead than who, or according to what standard. Who decided where you should be by now? Many women carry around invisible benchmarks that were never consciously chosen, yet they use them to judge themselves every day.

Comparison drains power quickly. So does resentment. The belief that "it's all on me" can feel incredibly heavy, even when no one has actually said that you have to carry everything alone. When we peel back the layers with curiosity, we often discover that this pressure is internal. It is a story we are telling ourselves. Both comparison and resentment give our power away, and both can leave us feeling broken or depleted, even when the numbers say otherwise.

The shift begins when you turn your attention away from what you think you lack and toward what you have been given.

Consider this a quick inventory of assets: talents, skills, interests, and resources. When you focus on developing these strengths and working within them, money decisions feel more grounded and less emotionally charged.

Settling Into the Right Lanes

I spent time in this resentment pattern myself, believing that everything was on my shoulders. During that period, my coach offered me a powerful reframe. Instead of thinking, "It's all on me," she encouraged me to think, "This is mine to do."

That shift felt empowering rather than burdensome. I could say, "I am the best person to make this decision. I am the best person to handle this task." The emotional weight lifted almost immediately.

There were times in my marriage when I felt like the finances rested entirely on me. Through coaching and reflection, I began to see something important. I actually was the best person for certain aspects of our financial life, and my partner was the best person for others. We each had different gifts and talents.

For example, I was excellent at earning money. My husband was terrific at making it grow. He was a stronger investor than I was. Once we recognized that, we settled into our lanes. I could say with confidence, "This is mine to do," and he could do the same. That clarity brought relief, balance, and a deeper sense of partnership. When ego loosens its grip, money stops feeling like a solo burden and becomes an intentional collaboration with yourself and others.

The Quiet Pull of Fear and the "Just One More" Cycle

Fear-driven thinking has a subtle way of shaping spending, saving, and even career decisions, especially for women who appear financially successful on the outside. Fear keeps you caught in a cycle of "just one more." *One more and then I will be happy. One more and then I can finally relax.* That "one more" can take many forms. One more handbag. One more zero on your retirement account. One more comment on your post. One more reward. One more title or promotion. All of these are external markers. They are about performance, validation, or reward. They are not about internal states like calm, confidence, or contentment. Happiness is always placed in the future rather than being available in the present. For example, consider purchasing an additional $3,000 handbag. While it may offer a temporary sense of satisfaction, it is crucial to recognize how this decision could delay a larger financial goal, such as building a safety net or contributing to a retirement account.

This is how fear-driven thinking quietly influences money. Sometimes it is quiet, and sometimes it is very loud. The voice of fear can be relentless. Living in fear-based overthinking and striving is exhausting, and it rarely gives your nervous system a chance to settle. Without that settling, contentment always feels just out of reach.

The antidote is gratitude. Gratitude is the gateway to contentment. When you can genuinely appreciate that your needs are met and recognize what is already working, ambition no longer has to feel heavy. You can still want more. You can still grow. But the striving softens, and the pressure eases.

When "Shoulds" Create Depletion Instead of Safety

Many high-achieving women are externally accomplished but internally depleted, and the word "should" plays a big role in that. "Shoulds" keep you locked in striving energy. You may look rich on paper, with titles, achievements, and tangible success, but you do not feel radiant. There is a difference between feeling rich and feeling radiant. Rich can be about accumulation and accomplishment. Radiant is about vitality, ease, and abundance that comes from within. When you are depleted, your energy dims. You can feel dull or flat, even in the midst of success. Radiance, on the other hand, carries an openness and abundance that is very different from scarcity.

The pressure of "shoulds" often leads to overwork and what I call "overing." It might be overworking, but it can also be over-scrolling, over-checking out, over-numbing, or even over-exercising. There are many ways this shows up. You know you are in it when it feels negative, when it feels draining, and when it leaves you more depleted than grounded.

When Success Follows the Wrong Script

I once worked with a client who was highly successful on paper but disconnected from her life. She had done everything right according to the rules she inherited. She earned the degrees.

She built a prestigious career. She checked all the boxes of what success was supposed to look like. And yet, she did not love the life she was living.

As we talked, it became clear that she had stopped listening to her own soul. She was not guided by the voice of love. She was following what I often call the "smart girl path." This is the path shaped by family expectations, cultural messages, and the belief that if something is not hard, you must be doing it wrong. For her, effort and struggle had become proof of worth. There was no sense of flow. Everything felt heavy, as if ease itself was suspicious.

Through coaching, we began to slow things down and uncover what she actually wanted. We explored her unique desires instead of inherited expectations. We mapped out a new path that honored her values rather than external definitions of success. A key part of that process was creating a safety net, so her nervous system could relax enough to imagine something different.

From there, we focused on visualization and embodiment. We looked at where she was headed and paid attention to what felt good in her body as she grew. We asked questions: *What feels aligned? Where is your soul guiding you? What kind of growth actually supports you?*

Today, she has built an incredible business that truly aligns with her values and desires. When she stepped off the smart girl path and began listening to her own voice of love, her goals became her own for the first time.

Boundaries as a Bridge from Ego to Soul

Boundaries play a powerful role in moving from ego energy into soul energy, and it all begins with clarity. Boundaries require you to know what you want and what you do not want. While it can be helpful to name what you do not want, the real work is staying focused on the column of what you do want. That is where soul energy lives. The challenge is keeping your attention there and not letting it drift into the ego's habit of negativity.

Ego energy is often loud and critical. It fixates on flaws, limitations, and everything you think you are not good at. That focus is heavy and draining. Soul energy is oriented toward your gifts. It speaks more truthfully to you. It moves you into mindful action. Even though this book is about finances and earning, this way of relating to boundaries applies to many areas of your life.

I like to visualize boundaries as a picket fence rather than a stone wall. A picket fence allows for connection, clarity, and choice. It is not about shutting people out. It is about knowing where you stand. As you do this work, you begin to get clear on what you want to offer and how you want to offer it.

For example, I love helping others, and I am very clear about the form that help takes. It rarely comes in the form of a cash gift, aside from generous tipping from time to time. As a debt-free landlord, I can support tenants with housing costs, but I stop short of offering them cash when they are going through a difficult season. That boundary lets me draw on love and soul energy instead of guilt or fear.

This comes up often with clients who are concerned about helping their parents financially. We talk a lot about what they want to provide for their parents with their time, money, and emotional energy as their parents age. We explore how to set those boundaries clearly and how to communicate what they can and cannot do. The same conversation applies to children as well, though I see more women today carrying deep concern about their parents.

What Emotional Wellness Around Money Really Looks Like

Emotional wellness around money goes far beyond simply feeling calm or less anxious. It comes down to determining your personal sense of "enough." This is why the math work earlier in the book matters so much. Without clarity around your numbers, it is easy to stay stuck in a cycle of more and more without ever knowing when you have arrived.

Knowing your "enough" means understanding your boundaries. It means asking yourself what is enough for you, not for your peers, your family, or your culture. It also means getting clear on what you want for your future self. That clarity creates emotional safety in a way that endless striving never can.

I learned this lesson personally when I accepted a promotion that came with a bigger title and more responsibility, but no increase in income. It did not take long for me to realize that it was an ego move, not a soul move. I stepped back into a part-time role so I could be with my children before and after school. That decision was deeply soul-aligned. I am incredibly grateful for those seven years of being present in that way.

From that point on, I began filtering my financial and career decisions through a different set of questions. *Does this align with my values? Does this align with my desires? How does my future self feel about this choice?*

Emotional wellness around money also involves the body. Moving your body in ways that cannot be measured or ranked can be incredibly healing. Practices like yoga, somatic movement, or even dance allow old emotions and fear to move through the body and be processed. When those emotions are released, they no longer silently influence your current decisions.

If you suspect that some of your goals are being driven by fear or obligation, the first step is surprisingly easy. You pause. You breathe. You feel. This is where mindfulness comes in. The HALT practice that I often return to begins with checking in with yourself in a very human way. Ask yourself, "Am I hungry, am I angry, am I lonely, or am I tired?" When one of those needs is present, it deserves care and attention first.

If none of those are at play, then you move to a deeper question. You gently ask, "What would love do?" And then you listen.

Listening is the key, because the voice of love is quiet. It is calm. It speaks in stillness. That is why we often have to intentionally turn the volume down on the ego to hear love clearly. This listening thrives in moments of silence. It could be through meditation, prayer, or a brief pause in your day where you prioritize presence over pressure. Saying, "I want to listen to the voice of love right now," opens up space for truth to emerge.

My hope for you is that you begin to feel both rich and radiant through love and abundance. That starts with learning to recognize the different voices guiding your choices. The voices of scarcity are the ones that leave you feeling less than, depleted, disconnected, discontent, or stuck in constant striving. They exhaust you. They keep you reaching without ever letting you arrive.

The voice of love is different. It is soul energy. It allows you to feel fulfilled while still growing. It challenges you without depleting you. It brings a sense of flow, guiding you toward mindful action and a life that feels expansive and aligned. This is the energy of splendor.

Financial wellness is a crucial part of this journey. Earlier, we focused on financial literacy. Now, we are stepping into financial wellness, the integration of numbers, emotions, values, and self-trust.

When love leads your financial choices, money becomes a tool for alignment rather than a source of pressure. It supports your well-being, your relationships, and your daily experience, leading you on a path to a life that feels abundant in every sense of the word.

KEY TAKEAWAYS

- Fear does not always look like avoidance. It often disguises itself as striving, comparison, and the pressure to prove yourself through money and achievement.
- When you shift from "it's all on me" to "this is mine to do," money decisions feel lighter, more grounded, and more collaborative.
- The "just one more" cycle keeps contentment out of reach. Gratitude brings your nervous system out of fear and allows ambition to soften without disappearing.
- Boundaries rooted in clarity and love protect your energy and help you give from alignment instead of guilt, fear, or obligation.
- Emotional wellness around money begins when you define your own sense of enough and learn to pause, listen, and ask what love would do.

CHAPTER FIVE

Mindful Money Mindset

Everyone has a money mindset. It is the story you carry about your ability to earn, manage, and grow money. It is also the silent driver in the background of your financial life. That quiet narrative influences how you show up to your money every single day. It shapes whether you build wealth, stay stuck, or feel conflicted and discontent, even when you earn well.

Our thoughts are sentences in our minds. Those sentences, when repeated over and over, consciously or subconsciously, become beliefs. Those beliefs then form your money mindset. Most of us rarely pause to examine our money thoughts. We do not ask where they came from. We do not question whether we even like them. And we seldom intentionally redirect them.

I like to think of your money mindset as a global positioning system. A GPS does not magically get you to your destination, but it does determine the direction you are heading. If you know you want to go somewhere but do not program the destination clearly, you can easily end up spinning in circles or traveling in the opposite direction altogether. This kind of aimlessness can lead to tangible financial consequences, like earning a high income year after year but finding yourself with no significant net worth to show for it. Without clear targets, even a comfortable paycheck may not translate into financial security.

The Beliefs That Sound Responsible but Keep You Small

When I work with high-achieving women, I often hear money beliefs that sound responsible on the surface, but actually limit growth. One common belief is, "I do not want more than my share." The challenge is that most women who say this have never defined what their share actually is. They have never decided what enough means for them.

Closely tied to this is a fear of being perceived as greedy. Some women go even further, adopting the belief that money is bad or that having more means taking something away from someone else. This ignores the reality of abundance. There is enough for everyone. And the more you earn or learn, the more you are often able to help others. Having money does not change who you are. It simply highlights it. The person you are before money is the person you will continue to be once you have it.

I also want to share something important here. Throughout this book, I often reference the flow of money, and I invite you to imagine it like a beautiful waterfall. As you learn and grow, let that water cascade to other women. Share what resonates and support each other to create a ripple effect.

The Quiet Confidence Killers

Many of the beliefs that keep women stuck do not sound responsible at all. They sound self-protective:

"I am bad with math."
"I do not know what to do."
"No one ever taught me this."

These thoughts drain confidence. They make capable, intelligent women doubt themselves and hesitate to engage meaningfully with their money. The goal is not to swing from negative beliefs straight into extremes like, "I am amazing with money." That kind of leap rarely feels believable.

Instead, we look for gentler, more honest shifts.

"I am willing to learn."
"I can figure this out."
"I can ask for help."

These beliefs move you out of self-judgment and into possibility. Over time, as you take small actions from this place, your confidence grows naturally.

I am not a huge fan of affirmations on their own. You have to believe them for them to work. And belief creates feeling. Feeling is what drives action. If an affirmation feels false, your nervous system knows it. Mindset work should create believable shifts that you can actually embody.

Rational Caution or Emotional Fear in Disguise

One of the most important skills you can develop with money is learning to tell the difference between a rational financial concern and an emotional fear that is pretending to be careful. The easiest way to know the difference is not in your head. It is in your body.

When I am coaching a client, I will often repeat back a single thought they have just said. Then I ask them to locate where it lives in their body (e.g., chest, stomach, throat, or elsewhere). Once they find it, I ask a simple question. *Does this feel positive or negative?*

When a concern is rational, it does not feel heavy or constricting. It tends to feel steadier. It often comes from a place of love, self-trust, or protection without panic. When it is emotional fear, it feels very different. It carries tension. It feels tight or urgent. This is usually the ego at work, the same fearful voice we talked about in the last chapter.

From there, we gently work with the sentence itself.

Do you like this thought?
Why or why not?
How does this thought serve you?
Who gets to decide what you think?

Sometimes we follow a version of the five whys, but the questions are not always why questions. They are curiosity-based. They are designed to help you pause and really examine the sentence you have been running unconsciously on autopilot.

One of the most beautiful parts of coaching is this moment. Parroting a thought back to yourself allows you to hear it clearly. Editing it gives you a choice. You get to decide how you want that sentence to feel in your body, and whether it actually moves you toward your financial desires or keeps you stuck.

The Sacred Pause and Your Nervous System

I love using the story of the wise old owl and the barking dog to explain what is happening in your brain when money stress shows up. The wise old owl represents your prefrontal cortex. This is the calm, logical, problem-solving part of your brain. It is often called the adult or evolved brain.

The barking dog represents your amygdala. This is where fear lives. Fight, flight, or freeze. It is the part of you that reacts when finances feel threatening or overwhelming.

When the dog starts barking loudly due to stress or a perceived financial threat, the owl flies away. Rational thinking shuts down. Calm responses disappear. You are left reacting instead of responding.

The sacred pause helps calm the dog.

Facts are incredibly important here. When you look at actual numbers and real information, it reassures the nervous system. The dog settles. When the dog is calm, the owl can return. And when the owl is present, you can access your incredible ability to problem solve, think clearly, and take mindful action with your money. From that place, your decisions feel grounded, intentional, and aligned with the life you want to create.

When Vigilance Masquerades as Responsibility

Many women believe that constant vigilance equals responsibility. But most of the time, it quietly robs you of emotional and mental rest. Money compounds over time. Sometimes the most responsible thing you can do is give it time to work.

We talked in the last chapter about "overing." Over-watching. Over-stressing. Over-checking. The question to ask yourself is simple. How is this actually helping right now?

I come from a farming family. We grew peaches and walnuts in orchards. When you plant those trees, you know it will take years before they produce fruit or nuts, same as investments. They do need seasonal care, like pruning and weeding, but it would be a waste of time and energy to check them every single day.

If you are checking your investment (different from cash flow) daily, you have to ask yourself where that impulse is coming from. Is it love or is it fear? Is it truly control, or the illusion that you can change the outcome faster by watching it closely?

Now, if we were growing radishes, that would be different. Radishes grow fast. You might check them every few days because you are expecting quick results. Money works the same way. Some parts of your financial life are long-term orchards. Others are short-term gardens.

The key question is this. What are you growing, and what is the best return on your investment of time and energy?

Most constant vigilance comes from fear, not love.

I know this personally. When I was preparing to exit my corporate job, I checked my 401(k) balance constantly. And when I got honest with myself, I realized it was my ego and fear driving that behavior. Is it going to be enough?

Once I noticed that, I gave myself permission to stop. I created a habit stack. If I wanted to check my investment account, I had to do a one-minute plank first. That one-minute pause was powerful. It made me ask myself, " Do I really want to check this? And what is actually going to change from yesterday?

Giving yourself and your money a break is good for your emotional health. That pause interrupts the "overing" behavior and brings you back into intention.

This does not mean ignoring your money. I absolutely believe in tracking and allocating your expenses so you stay current and organized. The right cadence depends on your life. It might be daily, weekly, or monthly. It depends on the volume of your transactions and what feels supportive rather than overwhelming. Your life changes. Your systems can change with it. The goal is awareness without obsession.

Emotional Rest, Mental Rest, and Financial Mindfulness

True security comes from the combination of emotional rest, mental rest, and financial mindfulness. Emotional rest often shows up first. My clients feel relief from worry and resentment when they have a financial plan and the money mindset to support it. A plan alone is not enough. The mindset that accompanies the plan is what allows you actually to feel supported by it.

Mental rest comes from knowing your financial facts. Your cash flow. Your numbers. Your financial independence number. When you know these, the overthinking begins to quiet. The constant number crunching and over-consuming of information fades.

Financial mindfulness is calm confidence. It is knowing that you will be okay. It is trusting yourself and your ability to earn, manage, and grow money through all seasons of life. Financial mindfulness means using your values and desires as filters for your financial decisions. It recognizes that money compounds, just like confidence does. You start with the facts. Then you ask yourself how you want to feel about them. Then you choose actions that align with both.

These three forms of rest are different, but they are deeply connected. And when they come together, they create the grounded, calm confidence that allows you to feel truly secure with your money.

When Money Fear Is Really About Worth

This situation comes up more often than people realize. A woman has made decisions in the past that did not turn out the way she hoped. Maybe she took her eye off the money. Maybe she gave her power away to a business or life partner because she believed they were more competent or more comfortable with numbers.

At first, it can feel responsible. Logical, even.

But over time, trust is lost. The money is not handled in alignment with her values, her money mindset, or her risk tolerance. And when the outcome is painful, the belief that forms becomes personal.

"I am not good with money."
"I cannot be trusted with this."
"This cost me."

What is really happening underneath is a wound to worthiness. I am thinking of several women as I share this, because the pattern is so similar. Like my family orchard, wealth requires seasonal maintenance and the belief that you are capable of tending to it. You are worth investing in. In fact, you and your amazing brain are often your best investment.

One woman came to realize that she never wanted to know the dollars and cents. She wanted someone else to handle it for her. After trust was broken and money was lost, she felt deep regret. What shifted was not suddenly learning complex financial formulas. What shifted was her awareness. She realized she actually did know enough. She knew what she wanted. She simply had not stepped into her power. She had made a conscious or subconscious decision to believe someone else was better at managing money than she was.

Another woman ran a successful professional practice with her spouse as her business partner. He handled the books. She focused on the work she loved. She did not review the profit and loss. She did not watch the growth. When the relationship ended, she was shocked to discover the financial reality. The business was sold, and she was left in a very different position than she expected at that stage of life. She discovered a self-worth gap. She had believed she was not capable of understanding money, and that belief shaped the outcome.

Another woman built a business with a partner that eventually went bankrupt. The partner took the money and left. She felt like a failure. She had been working hard, focused on growth, not realizing what was happening behind the scenes. The loss of trust and the experience of bankruptcy deeply impacted how she saw herself.

In all of these situations, the real shift began when the woman saw clearly that the fear was not about dollars. It was about believing she was not capable, not worthy, or not enough. Once that belief was brought into the light, everything changed.

Editing the Story That Shapes Your Financial Life

The thoughts you allow to run unchecked shape your money mindset. Most of us do not turn down the noise of life long enough to hear what we really think about money. When we do slow down, the answers can be surprising.

Sometimes I will ask women to complete a sentence. "Rich people are..."

If the answer is greedy, unethical, or evil, then of course, opportunities to build wealth feel unsafe. The subconscious does not want you to become someone you believe is wrong. Without realizing it, you begin to repel wealth. You push away opportunities because your beliefs are quietly protecting you from becoming someone you think you should not be.

This is why the sacred pause and mindfulness are so powerful. Your subconscious is always working, whether you are aware of it or not. When you slow down, listen, and create space, you can finally hear the sentences that have been shaping your financial life.

And then comes the most important work. Editing them. When you change the story, you change the direction. You stop spinning in circles. You stop walking away from what you actually want. You begin moving toward a relationship with money that feels grounded, intentional, and aligned with who you truly are.

KEY TAKEAWAYS

- Your money mindset is built from the sentences you repeat in your mind, and until you pause to hear them, they quietly direct your financial life without your knowledge.
- Beliefs that sound responsible or self-protective often come from fear, and gentle, believable shifts create real confidence and momentum.
- Learning to tell the difference between rational caution and emotional fear begins in the body, not the intellect, and curiosity creates choice.
- The sacred pause calms your nervous system, brings your facts back online, and allows you to respond to money with clarity rather than panic.
- Financial security grows from self-trust, awareness, and alignment. Editing your story changes your direction.

CHAPTER SIX

Clarity & Communication

Clarity with money starts before the conversation. It starts in your body, in your ability to feel grounded, present, and safe enough to speak honestly. With money, you play a few key roles, whether you realize it or not.

The first role is the observer. Think of this as the bird watcher, not the judge or the jury. This role is about noticing your thoughts, patterns, and behaviors around money without assigning blame or shame. When you pause long enough to hear the thoughts that are creating your money mindset or money story, you step into choice. This is where your power lives. You get to ask yourself, *"Do I like these thoughts? Do they support the relationship I want with money? Do they support the relationship I want with myself and with others?"*

The second role is the editor. This is the focus of this chapter. The editor looks at your money story and decides what stays, what changes, and what no longer serves you, so you can hold the vision of your future self.

The third role is the driver. Sometimes you drive alone. Other times, it's like driving a bus—you're responsible for others or carrying them with you for a time.

These three roles—observer, editor, and driver—form the quiet foundation of building wealth. We'll focus on editing and clear communication, because many people have not fully identified what is truly important to them. Once you do, communication naturally becomes kinder to yourself and others.

Rewriting Your Money Story

When I talk about rewriting your money story, I mean start by listening. Begin today: put pen to paper and start capturing your earliest memories. I ask my clients to write their first money memory. It could be earning, spending, managing, or simply hearing about money. From there, I encourage them to let it flow.

When I wrote my own money story, it started when I was twelve years old, and money was stolen from me at an ice rink. From that moment, it poured out onto seven pages filled with memories and people who shaped my relationship with money. The goal is to keep going and get it all out.

If you get stuck, prompts can help:

- *My first memory of money is…*
- *When it comes to money, I am…*
- *When I think of money, I think of this person because…*
- *When it comes to money, I am afraid of…*
- *My most influential time earning money was…*

These prompts are simply there to keep the story moving.

Once everything is out, clarify and edit. Remove unnecessary descriptions and replace them with specificity. For example, instead of a vague statement about a first job, write the exact number: My first job out of college paid $17,400 a year. Then, honestly, look at how you used that money, what you saved, and any debt you created. This step grounds you in reality.

Next, identify the emotions that come up from those facts. Are they positive, negative, or neutral? Where do you feel them in your body? If your emotions are neutral or positive, you may not need to make many edits. The areas that deserve your attention are the negative ones.

Ask yourself how you can shift those thoughts to feel less triggering or slightly more positive. Take a moment today to notice one negative thought about your finances and intentionally reframe it. Remember, you cannot create a positive financial result from a negative thought. When you shift the energy behind your thoughts, you shift the outcome.

The changes do not need to be dramatic. Small edits create powerful results. When your thoughts align with your desired outcome, your actions follow naturally. Clarity in thought and communication leads to a more intentional and aligned financial life.

The Sound of Silence

I often see high-achieving women silence themselves in money conversations to avoid perceived confrontation. Before the conversation, they play it out in their minds. They decide how it will go, how they'll be received, and whether they'll be discounted. Power is given away before a word is spoken. This shows up as staying quiet, minimizing concerns, or deferring to someone else's authority, even when something does not feel right.

I worked with a woman who was intimidated by her financial advisor. When we explored it, the reason was clear: This was the advisor her father had chosen years ago. She had not chosen him. She felt talked down to and uncomfortable asking questions. Despite her success, she remained in the role of daughter in this relationship.

Because of that dynamic, she avoided asking questions about her money, especially around fees. Conversations focused on desired outcomes but never on how she was actually getting there. She wanted her investments to align with her values, desires, and risk tolerance, but instead, she was handing everything over and hoping the results would match what she wanted.

When we slowed down and actually looked at her statements together, something she had never done before, I asked her some simple but powerful questions. *"Do you like how this is going? Do you like the relationship? Do you like the results you are getting? Do you like the fees you are paying?"*

Her answers gave her clarity. With clarity, she changed her approach. She chose to use email, which made her feel more grounded and confident. She asked direct questions. The dynamic changed, and so did her sense of alignment with her values and goals. She continued working with that advisor for a period of time, but now from a place of choice rather than obligation.

Just because someone has an opinion about your money does not mean you need to agree with it. Staying true to your values and desires is always more important than pleasing others or avoiding discomfort.

What Confident Money Communication Really Sounds Like

Confident money communication is rooted in self-trust, not control, perfection, or people-pleasing. And the guide here is curiosity.

Curiosity sounds like this: *"I may not know everything about finances yet, but I am willing to learn. I am willing to ask questions. I trust that I can figure this out."*

That mindset releases the pressure to be perfect or to have all the answers right away. It keeps you in your power. You stay in the driver's seat, choosing the route you want to take in building your wealth.

Confident communication is also grounded in facts. Ask questions like, *"What is the income here? What is the outcome? What is the actual flow of money?"* Facts give you something solid to stand on and help you make better decisions.

One clear sign that communication is not coming from confidence is the word "should." Confident money communication does not rely on "should" statements:

- "My partner *should* make more money."
- "My parents *should* stop telling me what to do with my money."
- "My manager *should* give me a raise."
- "My friends *should* stop asking me to go on expensive outings."
- "My sister *should* want to exchange holiday gifts."

These are all examples of expectations placed on others without clarity or ownership.

It is also worth noticing where you are "shoulding on" yourself. Expectations without facts or boundaries can drain your energy and create resentment.

Confident money communication focuses on what you can control: your mindset, your actions or reactions, and your energy. When you communicate from this place, conversations become clearer, kinder, and more aligned with your intentions.

Money as a Mirror

When women slow down and evaluate how they earn, spend, and save, awareness and clarity emerge. What they find is it's not about the money itself, but the feeling behind it. Our money actions are a mirror of our emotions. If you are feeling less than, you may act from scarcity. If you are feeling calm and confident, you tend to act from a place of love and abundance. Always check in with the energy and emotions behind your financial choices.

This awareness can reveal chosen or unchosen habits. For example, I realized I was a quantity-over-quality shopper. I did not like it. It created more stuff to manage, and an energetic drag—more things meant more decisions, clutter, and mental load. I slowed down and asked why those habits existed and whether they fit how I wanted to feel. They didn't. I felt like I was accumulating, not choosing intentionally.

I have coached many women who noticed a similar pattern. They go straight to the sales rack without pausing to clarify what they actually need or want. There is no specificity, just a reflex. That moment of pause is powerful because it brings you back into the realm of choice.

It also raises a deeper question. Why are we spending money in the first place? Is it about the item, or is it about the feeling we get from the experience? Sometimes money becomes a stand-in for comfort, connection, or even a hug.

I learned something else about myself when my husband jokingly called me a catch-and-release shopper. I would buy something, bring it home, and then realize I did not actually want it and return it, creating more work than fun. What I enjoyed was the outing, not the purchase. Once I saw that clearly, I could shift my behavior. Instead of buying things, I started intentionally creating outings I enjoyed. That shift made a big difference.

These insights extend beyond spending. Notice how you feel when your paycheck hits your account. Is there a rush? Do you even notice it? Do you feel excited, relieved, anxious, or indifferent?

What about saving? Do you feel good watching your savings grow toward a specific dream? Or have you not yet defined what that dream is?

Curiosity is key here. Tune in to how money makes you feel, not just what you do with it.

It can also be helpful to notice where you get your daily sense of reward. Where are you getting feelings of motivation, pleasure, or relief? Are those moments tied to money, or can they come from other areas of your life as well?

You do not need to overanalyze this. Just noticing creates awareness.

Why Couples Argue About the What but Avoid the Why

Every person enters a relationship carrying their own money story. Compassion is an important companion when money enters the conversation. No two people experience money the same way, even if they grew up in the same household.

You can have siblings raised under the same roof who develop completely different relationships with money. Each person brings their own successes, lessons, fears, and beliefs into a partnership. When couples argue about money, they are often reacting to these unseen stories rather than the dollars themselves.

Focusing only on what is being spent avoids the deeper conversation about why. The why requires vulnerability. It asks for understanding, curiosity, and a willingness to listen without judgment. Avoiding that conversation may feel safer in the moment, but over time, it erodes intimacy.

Simple prompts can open the door to a deeper connection. Questions like, "Tell me about the first paycheck you ever received and what you did with it?" help create dialogue. They move the conversation away from blame and toward understanding. From there, couples can begin dreaming together.

My husband and I have found that the best talks happen when we are forward-facing, both literally and emotionally. Walking together, holding hands, or sitting side by side in the car during what we call windshield time creates a sense of shared direction. Eyes on the horizon, not locked in a face-to-face debate.

Other helpful questions include:

- *What expectations do you have around money in this relationship?*
- *What does financial stewardship mean to you?*
- *How do you define generosity?*
- *Who was the most influential person in your life when it comes to money?*

These questions ignite compassion and understanding. From that place, couples can decide what parts of each money story they want to carry forward. They can take the successes, learn from the lessons, and create a shared vision. Dreaming together is where intimacy grows.

From Conflict to Connection

Our relationships are created by the thoughts we have about them. How you think about your partner and money directly shapes how you communicate and how you show up together financially.

One of the most powerful shifts couples can make is moving from "my" money or "your" money to simply "the" money. That subtle change neutralizes tension. Another option is to normalize each person's experience by mentally saying, *"Of course, someone with that money story would feel this way."* That kind of thinking opens the door to communication instead of conflict.

It is also important to pause and identify expectations. Expectations often hide in thoughts like, *"My partner should make more money."* Ask yourself, how is that thought helping you? Is it true? Is it motivating? Usually, it is not.

Couples can also benefit from identifying what truly matters to each of them. Rather than arguing about every expense, assign importance. For one person, buying organic food might be a 10 on a scale of 1 to 10, with 10 being the highest. It deeply aligns with their values. The kind of car they drive might be a three. For someone else, those numbers may be reversed. When couples see this clearly, they can align spending with shared values rather than argue over individual purchases.

This shifts the conversation from conflict to planning. Instead of asking, *"Why did you spend that?"* the question becomes, *"How fast do we want to reach our desired financial destination?"*

I am working with a couple who identified their financial independence number. They also know that investing in their children's education is a top priority. In alignment with their values, they chose to delay their financial independence timeline to focus on paying their children's current and future tuition. That decision did not feel like a sacrifice. It felt intentional. They understood the tradeoff, and they loved the choice they made.

Once you have the facts, you can ask a powerful question. Does this decision move us forward, keep us steady, or move us backward? Sometimes staying steady for a season is exactly the right choice.

Another piece of advice for couples is to allow some spending freedom. My husband and I found early on that having agreed-upon boundaries created safety and trust. When we first got married, we decided not to spend more than a certain amount without talking it through. That number was modest at the time, but it encouraged communication, boundaries, and joint decision-making.

Over the years, that number has grown along with our wealth, but the agreement remains. Not every couple combines finances, and that is okay. There is no single right way to manage money within a relationship. Some couples combine finances early and allow spending freedom within agreed boundaries. Others keep finances separate and find that works better for them. The only thing that matters is that the choice is intentional and aligned with your values and your relationship.

Clear is Kind

If you want to leave this chapter able to speak about money clearly, calmly, and without apology, the shift starts in your nervous system. Clear communication comes from being regulated, grounded, and connected to your heart center. When you are calm in your body, clarity becomes possible. As Brené Brown says, *"Clear is kind,"* and that is especially true with money.

This begins with normalizing your concerns. Of course, someone in your situation would feel this way. That simple acknowledgment reduces shame and softens resistance. From there, neutralization becomes powerful. Instead of framing conversations as "*my* money" or "*your* spending," shift to "*the* money" or "*the* spending." That language alone removes much of the emotional charge and defensiveness.

Another critical step is identifying where you are giving your power away, especially your emotional power.

I worked with a woman who had struggled to speak clearly about money throughout her marriage. After the relationship ended, she carried deep resentment toward her former husband. She blamed him for her financial situation, her lack of success, and even her happiness. Phrases like *"If it had not been for him, I would be wealthy,"* or *"His spending ruined my life,"* became part of her daily narrative.

What was striking was that they had been divorced for nearly twenty years. Yet she was still handing him power over her emotional and financial life. Her money story revolved around who he was, who he should have been, and what he took from her.

When you show up to your finances feeling miserable, the results reflect that emotional state. This is why personal responsibility matters. Not in a blaming way, but in an empowering one. Where are you giving away your emotional power by refusing to take ownership of your feelings? When you reclaim that power, your ability to communicate clearly changes immediately.

Clarity, curiosity, and compassion will serve you far better than defensiveness, deception, or discontent. Knowing what you want and how important certain experiences, feelings, or goals are to you, strengthens dialogue rather than shuts it down.

Please remember that everyone brings their own money story into the conversation. The goal is not to erase those stories, but to recognize the gifts within them and decide what you want to carry forward into your future. You are on the same team. Whether you are talking with a partner, a friend, or a financial advisor, approaching talks about money with a "let's build this together" mindset changes everything. It allows you to ask how you want to communicate and what feels supportive to you.

When you communicate clearly, you are not being difficult. You are being kind. Kind to yourself. Kind to your partner. Kind to your future. This kindness makes for better money conversations, deeper trust, stronger connection, and a financial life that truly reflects who you are and what matters most to you.

KEY TAKEAWAYS

- Clarity with money starts in your body, and being grounded and regulated makes honest communication possible.
- Observing your money story without judgment gives you choice. Editing that story with truth and specificity shifts both energy and outcomes.
- Confident money communication comes from curiosity and facts, not from "should" statements, avoidance, or people-pleasing.

- Money behaviors are a mirror of emotion, and pausing to notice the feeling behind earning, spending, and saving brings you back into the realm of intentional choice.
- Clear, neutral, and compassionate communication keeps you in your power and turns money conversations into opportunities for connection rather than conflict.

PART THREE

Thrive

Expand with Enjoyment

CHAPTER SEVEN

The Power of Vision

It's time to stop living on autopilot and start making choices with intention. You're capable and already know how to set and work toward goals. Sometimes, though, that motivation comes from fear, comparison, or obligation. Let's pause that cycle and try a new approach, one that comes from your heart. Trust your inner guidance to lead you. Earlier, we looked at your values and desires to find what truly motivates you. Now, those same values and desires can guide you toward the financial life you want.

A Plan Is Not the Same as a Vision

Once you decide to lead with your heart, the next question is: Are you building a plan or a vision? I love a good plan, and in my program, we create a Financial Freedom and Relief Plan. But a plan without a vision can still feel empty. When you infuse a plan with vision, you shift from seeking external approval to honoring deep internal alignment. A vision-driven plan becomes meaningful and alive, anchored in what truly matters to you. The difference between a successful plan and a fulfilling vision is where it starts. Plans made only with your head often reflect what others expect, shaped by society's ideas of success or messages about what you should want.

When we build your financial plan, we include your future self. We move from just thinking with our heads to listening to our hearts. Sometimes, this means letting go of old ideas or beliefs about what ambition or security should look like. For example, many women I work with have internalized scripts like *"I have to work harder than anyone else to be worthy,"* or *"Real security only comes from never spending a cent,"* or *"Ambition means climbing to the top, even if it doesn't feel true to me."* Naming and questioning these beliefs is a powerful first step. As you notice which of these old stories come up for you, permit yourself to revise or release them.

When I help a woman picture her future self, I notice something interesting. She often describes her life like we did when playing the board game Life as kids. She lists the markers: titles, a house, a car, degrees, diplomas, and family. It's like she's still moving her little car across the board, collecting symbols that show she's winning.

But what's often missing are the feelings and energy, the inner signs of success. That's why we focus on what's already good in your life and where you're headed. Positive emotions become your fuel as you drive forward, helping you spot new opportunities along the way. It can feel like finding small gold nuggets that guide you toward your best outcome.

Moving Beyond External Markers

The next step is learning how to tap into this new energy. Helping someone move beyond outside measures of success starts with pausing, breathing, and noticing how you feel. In one-on-one coaching, I often share my belief in her until she can believe in herself. Sometimes, she needs to borrow my confidence in her ability to create a vision.

We use a simple breathing exercise: inhale for 7 counts, hold, then exhale for 7 counts. We might do this three times, and it helps us feel grounded. It quiets outside noise and brings us back into our bodies. From there, she can look inward.

Next, I ask her to make a list of things she truly loves. If she's 30, I suggest 30 things. I did this myself at 50, writing my list during a plane flight. I still look at it because it shows who I am in a way no title can. That list might include experiences, objects, places, people, or rituals. For example, I love a good journal, a soft cashmere throw, and a favorite pen. When I see these things together, they give me a feeling, like a warm hug.

One client, after making her list, pictured the Himalayas. Another saw a beach at sunset. Someone else imagined a forest. Each image became a symbol of her energy. Once you have your image, it becomes a helpful filter for decisions on your financial freedom journey. *Does this request match my image? Does this demand fit? Does this purchase reflect it?*

If something feels like a warm hug, I say yes. It supports my financial wellness and matches my path to building wealth. It honors my top values. If it doesn't feel like that warm hug, I say no. When I think about this book, it feels like a warm hug, and that's how I know it's right for me. Your vision will feel that way, too. It won't just look good on paper, it will feel good in your body.

Ditching Discipline for Devotion

Accessing your energy is only the beginning. Real change happens when you choose to act from that place. Living in your head might feel natural because you've been taught to be disciplined. Discipline isn't bad, and it has probably helped you achieve a lot. But when you imagine your future, discipline alone isn't enough. It can even keep you from the energy that makes your journey fulfilling and radiant.

I often have to say, *"Wait a second. Let's move out of the head, where discipline and willpower dominate, and move down into the heart, where devotion lives."* We begin with grounding. We slow the breath. We center the body. This takes less than ten minutes. When the breath slows down, the nervous system softens.

From this grounded place, we focus on devotion to your future self and where you want to go, both financially and personally. You might picture yourself five, ten, or even twenty years from now. Then, use your senses. What does your future self smell, taste, or feel on her skin? What does she see around her? What sounds help her relax? What's her favorite scent, drink, or piece of clothing? Where is she? What is she doing that makes her feel true to herself?

When you use your senses, your vision becomes something you can actually feel in your body. This is mindfulness in action. Once you've experienced that version of yourself, we start building the plan.

Making Starting, Stopping, and Continuing Clear

On any journey, things will change. Life brings new situations, different seasons, and surprises. That's when your personal filter comes into play. When you've created a vision from your heart like a warm hug, a sunset beach, a mountain, or a forest, you can come back to it. It becomes your guide. When you face a decision, ask yourself: "*Will this feel good in five years? In ten? Will it matter in fifteen? Does it move me closer to where I want to go, or further away?*"

You don't need to overthink it. Sometimes, just checking in with yourself is enough.

Next, take stock of your life. What's working and helping you reach your goals? Keep doing that. What isn't working or is pulling you off track? Stop that. What could help you move forward? Start that.

It's rarely one big gesture that changes your financial life. It's the small, consistent, mindful actions over time. Sometimes, what needs to stop is internal, like self-doubt or old negative beliefs. Once you notice thoughts that don't help you, you can interrupt them. You might say, *"I no longer think that about myself. I no longer believe I am bad with money. I notice every day the ways I am making positive choices that move me toward the results I want."*

You start to notice your own growth. Then you put what you've learned into action. Wisdom means using what you know. Sometimes, that means picking just one thing at a time: brainstorm, choose one, try it, see what happens, and adjust as needed.

Having a vision makes it easier to know what to start, stop, or keep doing. You're choosing in line with the future self you've already imagined. Yet, many high-achieving women still default to an old pattern. I once had a client who came to a session feeling completely overwhelmed. Her to-do list felt endless. She was spinning in worry about how much there was to do, and that spinning kept her stuck. Instead of moving forward and completing tasks, she was circling them in her mind.

When we looked closer, I saw her usual pattern as a high achiever. She would rely on discipline, telling herself to push harder and power through. That kind of energy comes from the head and depends on willpower. But many of the tasks on her list weren't things she actually wanted to do.

We paused and wrote everything down. Something surprising happened: some tasks didn't need to be done at all, she could delegate others, and some she could finish much faster with a little focus.

Then we shifted her energy. First, we noticed what discipline felt like in her body. Next, we softened into dedication. Finally, we found devotion in her heart. She realized she was truly devoted to her business and the direction she wanted to go. When she felt that devotion, something changed. Instead of forcing herself to do tasks just because she thought she should, she chose to do them because they mattered to her.

We've been taught that if something isn't hard, we must be doing it wrong. Discipline is often seen as the only way to succeed. But when we work from devotion and lead with our hearts, the energy changes completely. The work still gets done, but it happens more gently and with more enjoyment. In the end, you're not just checking off tasks; you feel proud, and that pride helps you feel abundant instead of drained.

As she shifted into devotion, I could literally see the change in her body. Her shoulders dropped. Her eyes softened. She looked at her list again and said, *"I know exactly what my next step is. I have stepped off the overwhelmed spinning wagon, and I am now on the road to getting these tasks completed."* The tasks no longer felt like proof of her inadequacy. They became expressions of her commitment to her vision.

Live It Now, Not Someday

I encourage you to begin living a rich and radiant life today. Have a conversation with yourself about who your future self truly is. Tune into what she smells, tastes, feels, sees, and hears.

Reconnect with the emotional energy of her life, and you will experience small pieces of that now.

I am not suggesting that you go into debt to buy a car you cannot afford or overhaul your wardrobe. This is about blooming into that version of yourself. If your future self feels calm and confident, you can practice those qualities now. If she feels grounded and radiant, allow yourself to embody that energy now, regardless of your bank account balance. This is where the idea of a rich and radiant life truly comes alive. You stop postponing the feeling until someday. You start living it today.

We have been conditioned to use pain as motivation. We tell ourselves that struggle is proof we are doing it right. If it is not hard, I must be failing. So many high-achieving women operate from that belief. They feel they must outwork everyone, be the best in the class, and prove their worth through discipline.

But what if we chose to lead with our hearts instead?

I was recently reflecting on a gold medal performance in Olympic figure skating. I am not an expert in skating, but what struck me was not her technical precision. It was her joy. The performance obviously came from the heart center. And it earned the gold.

That's the shift I want you to make in your financial life. Create experiences that feel abundant from the inside out. That kind of life comes from living in line with your values and desires. Sometimes, that means saying no to what society expects or waiting to buy things until you can truly afford them. I've felt the difference myself. A vacation on a credit card brings stress, but one paid for in advance brings peace. One leaves your future self worried, the other honors her.

Consider your future self in your decisions today. Turn off autopilot and be intentional. Use a calm mind to choose wisely rather than react from fear. Lead with love. Choose devotion over discipline. Make small, mindful decisions consistently. Trust that the woman you are becoming is already guiding you home.

KEY TAKEAWAYS

- Turn off autopilot and choose a vision rooted in your heart, then build your financial plan around the future self you have already felt in your body.
- Use your vision as a filter for decisions by asking whether each choice aligns with your values and feels like a genuine yes from within.
- Replace rigid discipline with devotion so your actions are fueled by love for where you are going rather than fear or obligation.
- Simplify growth by continuing what supports your future self, stopping what does not, and starting one small, consistent action at a time.
- Begin living your rich and radiant life now by embodying the energy, calm, and confidence of your future self in the choices you make today.

CHAPTER EIGHT

Permission to Prosper

I believe playing small helps no one. Hiding our strengths and potential serves neither us nor others. I picture a beautiful cathedral with stained glass windows meant to brighten the whole space. When those windows are dirty, their vibrant colors cannot shine through. The sun shines outside, but the window's radiance is hidden.

Many high-achieving women live this way without even realizing it. Their brilliance is there. Their gifts are there. Their ambition and capability are there. Still, something is dulling the light.

This chapter is about cleaning those windows and giving yourself permission to let your radiance shine. Only you can truly grant that permission. Yet I see so many women come to me looking for exactly that. They want someone to tell them it is okay to prosper, be ambitious, and want more.

Prosperity, however, is not something that someone else grants you. Prosperity is an intentional choice, and it's much bigger than money. Income is only one measurement of success. A prosperous life can also be rich with experiences, relationships, and meaningful moments. A life of splendor is not defined by income alone.

At one point, I intentionally stepped back from my career, moving from full-time to part-time for seven years so I could be with my children before and after school. Those hours were priceless for my family. I still built wealth in a part-time role, but made a choice that benefited my family. That decision let me align work and life with what mattered most. Sometimes, prosperity means stepping forward boldly. Other times, it means stepping back with intention. Both are expressions of a truly prosperous life.

What Permission to Prosper Really Means

In practical terms, permission to prosper means allowing yourself to fully own the success you have worked so hard to create. This is often not as easy as it sounds. I have seen many women hide their success or minimize it. I actually grew up with a perfect example of this.

In 1974, my mother became one of the first female criminal investigators. She worked for a district attorney's office, and at the time, women were almost never in those roles. If she was not the very first woman in California to hold that position, she was certainly among the first.

My mother had graduated from the police academy. Even dressed in heels, a skirt, and full makeup, she always had a badge, a gun, and handcuffs in her purse. She broke barriers every day simply by doing her job.

Yet almost no one knew since she didn't wear a uniform. To the world, she was just a mom. Maybe people thought she had an office job. They did not know what she was really doing or the impact she was having.

My mother passed away in 1994 after twenty years in that career. At her funeral, the church was completely full. She was given a full police funeral, and many people came to speak with me afterward. Former district attorneys and colleagues shared stories about the cases she had worked on and the people she had helped. She specialized in investigating rape, child molestation, and child abuse. This was incredibly difficult and important work.

After hearing these stories, so many people came up to me and said the same thing.

"I had no idea. I had no idea that's what your mom did all these years."

She had done remarkable work, but she rarely talked about it or allowed others to see the magnitude of what she had accomplished.

That experience showed me it's important to prosper and let your light shine because it benefits both you and others by being an example of what is possible, while diminishing your light serves no one.

My mother also gave me a piece of advice that shaped my thinking for years. A few months before she passed away, I had just started what I considered the beginning of my professional career. I was hired into a sales role at a Fortune 50 company. When I told my mother about the job, she said something that surprised me. She said, *"Oh no, this is not good. You do not want to make more money than your husband. It will upset the marriage."*

She said this not because she wasn't proud of me. She spoke from her own experience and fears. She was trying to protect me as she understood it. But in doing so, she unknowingly passed that fear to me.

For years after that conversation, part of me believed I needed to slow down and regulate my ambition. I thought I should not prosper too much, especially not more than my husband. I carried that story quietly as I built my career. And that belief helped no one. It did not benefit my husband and family. It did not benefit my employer. It certainly did not benefit me. In fact, it created more stress.

Over time, I realized I needed to unwind that story. I recognized that my mother shared her truth, which wasn't necessarily mine. This is why our work on money mindsets centers on unlearning beliefs we've held onto. We must regularly question old advice and decide if it still serves us today.

My hope is that, as you read this book, you reflect on your beliefs about money, success, and ambition. Consider which stories you have inherited, and give yourself permission to revise them.

Where Guilt About Wealth Begins

It's common for women to feel responsible for everyone around them, including their parents, partners, colleagues, and, often, their entire community. Over time, this deep sense of responsibility can quietly evolve into guilt.

Guilt around wealth often comes from both generational and cultural influences. I have coached many women, particularly firstborn daughters, who feel an unspoken expectation to take care of everyone. That expectation can feel very heavy. Sometimes it was never even spoken out loud, yet it still shapes the way they move through the world.

I once asked a client a very simple question. I asked her, *"Who told you that you are supposed to be doing all of this?"* She paused and thought about it for a moment before answering. Finally, she said, *"No one. I just felt like I was supposed to."*

She felt like she was carrying everything. When responsibility feels like a burden, it gradually drains the energy and fulfillment out of what we do. I experienced this pattern, too. At one point, my internal narrative was: *It is all on me. Everything rests on my shoulders.* That thinking quickly led to burnout.

I had to change how I thought about my responsibilities. Instead of thinking everything was on me, I chose a more empowering narrative. I started telling myself, *"This is mine to do."* The phrase might not resonate with everyone, but for me, it transformed the experience from feeling overwhelmed to feeling empowered.

It reminded me that I was choosing this role and that I could carry it.

Another thought I began practicing was this: *I am the best one for this job (or task).* Thinking this way made me grateful to use my gifts and talents meaningfully.

Reframing Ambition

Ambition is one of the most misunderstood qualities in women. I believe this is one of the most important cultural shifts happening today. We are still learning to see ambitious women in a positive light. It is easy to forget how new many of these opportunities are. Women's access to high-income, influential positions and leadership roles is still relatively recent.

When I began my career in 1994, there were no female Fortune 500 CEOs. While some had held these positions before, at that moment, there were no visible women leaders at the top of business, nor were there clear role models. Today, the number has grown but remains small. Only recently did female Fortune 500 CEOs reach around ten percent, or about 50 women, leading major companies.

I never personally aspired to become a Fortune 500 CEO, but that statistic tells us something valuable. When women can see other women leading, earning, and expanding their influence, what feels possible changes.

Unfortunately, ambitious women are still often misunderstood. They are frequently labeled as cold, selfish, or self-centered. In my experience, women bring powerful qualities to leadership. They bring heart-centered leadership, emotional intelligence, and a deep awareness of values and alignment.

Earlier in this book, we talked about filtering decisions through your values. Ambition can work the same way. When ambition aligns with your values, it becomes a force for growth and contribution.

Your body will tell you when ambition has gone too far. If it produces a net negative in your life or in your body, something is out of alignment. We cannot create a positive outcome from ambition fueled by negative intention.

But when ambition comes from alignment and purpose, it becomes a form of service. That service is not only for others; it is also for yourself. I think it is important to say this clearly, because many women have learned to think that everything they do must benefit others. Healthy ambition honors both.

At the end of every yoga class I teach, I close with a simple phrase that reflects this belief. I say, *"May your light guide you and others to the greatest good."*

Learning to Spend Without Guilt

Purpose-driven ambition often leads to a surprising next step: learning how to receive and enjoy prosperity! I once worked with a client who felt intense resistance to spending money on herself. For a long time, she had been focused on paying down her student loan debt. She was incredibly disciplined and worked very hard to eliminate it. Eventually, she succeeded. The debt was gone, and financially, she was in a strong position. But internally, the old survival story was still running.

Part of her still believed, *"I do not deserve this."* Her sense of self-worth was tangled up in years of striving and pushing through difficulty. Even though her financial reality had changed, her emotional relationship with money had not yet caught up. Her mind would constantly generate negative "what if" scenarios. *What if something went wrong? What if she spent money and later regretted it? What if she needed it later?*

All of her what if questions were focused on fear.

I asked her a different question.

What if things could be amazing? What would be amazing?

At that point in her life, it was time for her to step out of survival energy and even out of the intense strive energy that had driven her for years. It was time for her to step into thriving. Thriving includes greater ease, more enjoyment, and the freedom to experience the prosperity you have worked so hard for.

So part of our work was helping her reconnect with her body and feel safe again. Safe enough to recognize that she was no longer in survival mode. Safe enough to release some of the intense discipline that had defined her life for so long. We defined guardrails together so she could stay within the structure of her spending plan while also giving herself permission to enjoy her money.

It took time for her nervous system to adjust and for her mindset to shift. But eventually something beautiful happened, and she started spending money on herself. She went on a few weekend trips. She began doing things that genuinely brought her joy. At one point, she told me something that made me smile. She said she had been asking herself, *"What would be amazing?"*

She said it would be amazing to have a new bathtub she could truly enjoy. So she remodeled her bathroom into a space that felt luxurious and relaxing to her. Before, she would have immediately dismissed that idea with the thought, *"It's not necessary, and I didn't earn this. I do not deserve it."* Instead, she gave herself permission. Watching that shift happen was fun for me and incredibly rewarding for both of us.

Sprinkling the Gold Dust

When a woman improves her financial situation, the impact rarely stops with her. The ripple effect spreads outward to everyone around her. Women are historically generous. Research shows that women are about forty percent more likely to give and consistently give more. I see this even in my own household. My husband and I make decisions about our family giving together, and I am usually the one lobbying to increase the amount.

Financial expansion also creates emotional spaciousness. When women are no longer carrying the constant weight of financial stress or worry, their presence changes. They move through the world differently. They bring calm confidence, clarity, and radiance to the spaces they enter. They are admired not only for their achievements or their possessions. They are admired for their presence. Being around them feels uplifting.

Money mindset work often creates that kind of shift. I sometimes think of it as taking a golden vitamin for radiance. The women who do this work leave shimmering gold dust along the path for other women to follow. When one woman allows her light to shine fully, the whole room becomes brighter.

Generational Wealth Versus Legacy Wealth

That ripple effect is what eventually leads us into a much larger conversation about legacy wealth. When I explain the difference between generational wealth and legacy wealth, I often use a metaphor that is very personal to me. I grew up as a farmer's daughter. While my mother worked in law enforcement, my father was a farmer. More specifically, he was an orchardist.

Because of that background, I think about wealth in terms of trees. Generational wealth is often described as passing resources down a family line, as if nurturing a single family tree. That image is powerful, but it can also be limiting. It focuses entirely on one family.

Legacy wealth, on the other hand, is more like planting an entire orchard. If you are an orchardist, you would never plant just one tree and hope that all the fruit and all the benefits would come from that one source. You plant many trees. I have always loved the symmetry of an orchard. The rows of trees working together create something far more resilient and abundant than a single tree ever could.

Legacy wealth certainly includes financial wealth, and it absolutely supports your own family. But it also expands outward through the seeds you plant in your community and the people you influence along the way. Legacy wealth encompasses character, leadership, wisdom, generosity, and the example you set for others.

When people talk about generational wealth today, the conversation often stays focused on financial inheritance. Legacy wealth, by contrast, is the ripple effect of your time, your energy, your attention, and your leadership. The idea is that if you want a thriving village, you must also be a villager. That means serving your community, participating, and contributing. It might look like serving on a community board, supporting a scholarship, mentoring someone younger, or showing up for others in memorable ways.

I see women who have done their money mindset work naturally step into this kind of leadership. When women become financially secure and emotionally grounded around money, they often become powerful examples of what is possible for others. That is why I am so passionate about teaching legacy wealth.

Clean Generosity

An important idea I teach in legacy wealth is something I call clean generosity: giving without strings attached or with very clear direction.

For example, I once worked with a woman who inherited money from an uncle when she was 27. The inheritance was significant, around five hundred thousand dollars, and it came completely out of the blue. There were no instructions attached to it. There were no conversations about why it had been given or what the uncle hoped it would accomplish. The money simply appeared in her life after his death.

Instead of feeling excited or grateful, she felt overwhelmed. The money felt heavy. She did not want anyone to know about it. She did not know what to do with it. Without any context or intention behind the gift, it created more emotional weight than freedom.

Together, we began exploring what she wanted the money to represent in her life. What would feel aligned with her values and her vision? Once she began creating that clarity for herself, the gift became lighter and more meaningful.

I have also seen the opposite situation, where a gift is given with extremely rigid instructions. Another client inherited farmland from a family member who told her, "Never sell this."

That might sound like a simple instruction, but it was an enormous burden. Times change. Circumstances change. To place the word "never" on a financial gift can create pressure and guilt that lasts for generations.

Clean generosity allows a gift to become what it was always meant to be: an opportunity, not an obligation.

Living Your Legacy Now

One of the most powerful ways to build legacy wealth is to start living it today. A practical way to do that is by having a category in your monthly cash flow plan dedicated to generosity. Some people call this tithing. Others label it love, kindness, or giving.

When generosity is part of your spending plan, you begin creating a legacy in real time. I worked with a client who decided she wanted to support her niece's future education. Instead of waiting for some distant future, she created a dedicated investment fund within her portfolio for that purpose. The fund was still in my client's portfolio, and she maintained full control of it. But in her mind, she knew exactly what that particular fund's ticker symbol represented; it was connected to her niece.

Every time she added money to that fund, she knew she was building something for her niece's future. She even arranged for the fund to name her niece as beneficiary, ensuring that if something unexpected happened, the proceeds would still serve the purpose she intended. What I loved about this approach is that it allowed her to live her legacy now. She did not wait until the end of her life to make an impact.

Enjoying the Journey to Prosperity

I invite you to think about financial freedom the same way you might plan a vacation. For many of us, the vacation itself is only part of the joy. There is excitement in planning it, in imagining it, and in anticipating the experience. We enjoy becoming the person who is about to go on that trip. Then we enjoy the vacation itself, and afterward we carry the memories with us.

A rich and radiant life can unfold in the same way.

Financial freedom is not only something that happens someday in the future. It is a journey that can be enjoyed before, during, and after. There is joy in the planning, anticipation, and in becoming the person who lives with intention and clarity around money.

So many people dread this work. They avoid looking at their finances or delay making decisions that would move them forward. If you are not happy with the results you have today, that is not a failure. It is just an invitation to check in with the thoughts and energy that are driving your choices. Are those thoughts aligned with your values? Is your ambition creating a positive force in your life, or is it creating a net negative?

Sometimes the work involves cleaning up the past. It may mean paying off old debts or unwinding old stories that have been holding you back. For a season, that might require some strive energy. But the important question is how long you want to stay there.

We are living in a new era for women. Our access to money, leadership roles, and opportunity has expanded in ways that previous generations could only imagine. Yet I see many women staying in that heavy striving energy longer than they need to.

This book itself is part of my legacy wealth. It is my way of planting seeds for others. As you move forward, please carry this perspective with you. When you are intentional with your mindset and your energy, your actions start to align with the life you truly want. And when that happens, something beautiful occurs. The light that was always inside you finally shines through. Just like the stained glass windows of a cathedral, once the glass is clean, the radiance is never in question. The only question was whether you would allow it to shine.

KEY TAKEAWAYS

- Prosperity begins when you stop waiting for permission and allow yourself to fully own the success, opportunities, and life you are capable of creating.
- Many beliefs about money and ambition were inherited. Your work is to notice those stories, question them, and decide which ones deserve to shape your future.
- Ambition aligned with your values becomes a force for service, leadership, and meaningful contribution.

- Thriving means allowing yourself to move beyond survival and constant striving into enjoyment, ease, and appreciation for the life you are building.
- Legacy wealth is not just what you pass down. It is the generosity, leadership, and example that ripple outward and brighten others' paths.

CHAPTER NINE

Rich & Radiant: Living Your Freedom Plan

Being rich and radiant is a lifestyle you practice. It is the way you move through your financial freedom journey, rooted in three essential elements that work together over time: awareness, clarity, and vision. You have seen these before, but here is where they come together.

Awareness begins with understanding your values and recognizing your uniqueness. You must be honest about where you are today. That includes your numbers, your cash flow, your net worth, and your "math of the moment." It also includes the story you are telling yourself about money, your capabilities, and what is possible for you. Your mindset is shaped by that story, and whether you realize it or not, that story is either creating momentum or resistance in your life.

Clarity is the next step. It means getting clear on what you truly desire, not what you think you should want or what others expect, and understanding the energy needed to realize those desires. That energy is often driven by your internal narrative. Ask yourself whether your story is true and whether it generates positive, supportive energy that moves you forward. If your story is full of doubt or limitation, it will be difficult to create the results you want.

Vision brings everything together. You begin to see yourself as someone who follows through with confidence. You trust your ability to earn, manage, and spend money intentionally. Your vision shapes daily decisions, which ultimately determine your financial life as small choices compound over time.

This became very real for me in my own financial freedom journey. When I first started, I did not have a mentor. I was figuring it out as I went, and looking back, I can see that I made it harder than it needed to be because I did not initially include mindfulness in my approach.

What I did have, though, were three very clear desires. At the time, my children were just two and five years old, and I knew what I wanted for our future. I wanted to provide them with a college education. I wanted to live completely debt-free, including paying off our mortgage. And I wanted to build enough passive income to make work optional. I set a 20-year timeline, and my husband and I were aligned in working toward those goals together.

We wrote those three desires down to guide every financial decision. Each time, we asked whether a choice moved us forward, kept us in place, or set us back, sometimes intentionally stepping back for our values. For example, when our son wanted to attend a private high school, we adjusted our plans because we'd only prepared for college costs, but we made it work because it fit our values. My husband and I also took self-funded sabbaticals, possible only because we built a strong foundation by living below our income and committing to being debt-free.

As our income grew and we began receiving larger lump sums through bonuses, commissions, and even an inheritance, we knew we needed a simple, consistent way to handle them. We created a system that allowed us to enjoy our money while still prioritizing long-term growth.

We decided that 10% would be used for enjoyment. This was money we could spend freely without overthinking it or feeling guilty. Another 10% was allocated to giving, whether that meant supporting others, contributing to our children's future, or simply using it in a way that felt meaningful. The remaining 80% was invested so our money could work for us.

This structure made decision-making easier regardless of the amount of money that came in or where it came from. It removed the pressure of having to figure out what to do each time and replaced it with a system that supported both enjoyment and growth. Over time, it also reinforced the habit of putting our money to work in a consistent and intentional way.

Of course, not every investment worked out perfectly. There were mistakes along the way and choices that did not produce the results we expected. But even with those setbacks, we continued moving forward. The system kept us grounded, and the consistency of our actions kept us on track.

Ultimately, this path leads to a destination, and that destination can be defined by a number. It is your financial independence number, the amount that allows you to make work optional and the freedom to choose how you spend your time and energy.

When Math, Mindset, and Soul Come Into Alignment

To truly live this way, your math, mindset, and soul need to be aligned. When they are, you feel intentional. You feel organized. And at the same time, you feel alive with a sense of calm confidence. There is an ease that comes in, even though life is still life.

Alignment doesn't mean you won't face setbacks; you will, but you won't stay stuck. I picture this as a triangle: each side supports the others, making it one of the strongest shapes. Your math, mindset, and soul together create balance and stability. None overpowers the others; they continuously bring you back into alignment. This alignment allows you to experience a new level of harmony in how you earn, spend, and give. It no longer feels like something you have to constantly manage or control. This is where strong processes and a positive money mindset come together to create a centeredness, even when unexpected or challenging circumstances arise.

The structure comes from your financial plan. You make clear decisions about how your money will be used, then build systems around them. Automations are a big part of this. They allow your plan to operate in the background, so you don't have to keep making the same decisions. This reduces stress and frees up your energy for other areas of your life.

I encourage you to revisit your plan seasonally. And when I say seasons, I also mean the seasons of your life. The version of you who is just starting her financial journey has very different needs and priorities than the version of you who is further along. Your plan needs to evolve as you evolve.

And just as your plan evolves with the seasons of your life, so does the mindset that supports it. There is a belief I love that says you cannot create a positive outcome with a negative income. Your mindset matters more than most people realize. Many of us carry money stories we inherited or absorbed over time, without ever questioning them, which shape our decisions and results. You need to become aware of that story. Give yourself the space to pause and listen to what is actually playing in your mind. Once you can hear it, you can begin to shift it. Not all at once, but little by little. This is a process, and it takes time. It certainly did for me. But as you change your mindset, you start to see opportunities that were always there but that you could not recognize before. Opportunities for career growth, investment, and expansion. You feel lighter. The heaviness that once surrounded your money begins to lift.

Gratitude and appreciation play a huge role in this. When you cultivate gratitude, you raise your energy. You become more open, more receptive, and more magnetic. You place yourself in a position to receive.

When Your Plan Becomes Your Peace

Once you have a financial freedom plan in place, it becomes clear, accurate, and grounded in facts. You are no longer guessing. You are working within a system that is both manageable and measurable. That system creates guardrails, and those guardrails give you a sense of safety. Decisions that once felt heavy and overwhelming now feel simple.

One of the biggest transformations I see is the release of self-doubt and shame. There is a lightness that replaces the constant questioning. Instead of wondering if you are doing it right, you trust yourself. There is less friction in your day-to-day life and so much more mindfulness in how you move through your decisions.

The Ripple Effect of Financial Freedom

When a woman reaches this level of alignment, it changes how she shows up for everyone around her. It increases compassion for herself, family, friends, and the community. She becomes more understanding, more present, and more connected to the people in her life.

There is also a noticeable change in energy and generosity. When you are no longer operating from fear or scarcity, you have more to give. Women in this place often turn into more proactive problem solvers. They see opportunities to support others in ways they may not have considered before. For example, one woman I worked with planned a special trip to support her mother, who was running in the Boston Marathon. When your finances are aligned with your values, your generosity becomes more intentional and an extension of who you are.

Real Rich and Radiant Moments

I have had the privilege of witnessing many women step into their rich and radiant lives, and each story is unique, but they all share a common thread of transformation.

One woman came to me wanting to feel confident in her finances before getting married. She had a strong desire to enter the next chapter of her life with clarity and independence. Together, we worked through her financial picture, and she decided to become completely debt-free before her wedding day. Watching her follow through on that plan was incredibly powerful. By the time she walked down the aisle, she knew exactly what she was bringing into that partnership, and she felt grounded in her decisions.

Another woman had been in the same career for a long time. On paper, everything looked fine, but something no longer felt aligned. Through our work together, she began to recognize that her role was not supporting the location-independent life she wanted to create. She gave herself permission to explore new opportunities, even though it felt uncertain. What followed was a transition to a fully remote position that better aligned with her values, along with a $60,000 increase in annual income.

I also worked with a woman who was entering a new season of life and intentionally slowing down her career. She carried a lot of worry and self-doubt about what that would mean financially. As we worked through both the math and the mindset and brought her values into the conversation, she was able to let go of that fear. She moved from a place of concern into a place of adventure. She developed a calm confidence in knowing that she could handle whatever came next. She trusted herself in a way she had not before.

One Bouquet at a Time

When I think about what it means to live a rich and radiant life now, after everything I have experienced and learned, I come back to this: It is the small things that add up to big changes. It truly is the best compounding investment there is.

Over time, I have found that I desire less, I give more, and I focus on creating and curating meaningful experiences. I choose to see the best in others. There is something awesome about choosing to see the best in people and asking, *"How can I uplift someone today?"*

For me, one of those expressions has been growing and sharing dahlias. During harvest season, I make a point of giving bouquets to people in my everyday life. My neighbors, my doctor, my hairdresser, the post office clerk, the librarian, and the person at the coffee stand. I try to share a bouquet each day. I even buy cases of mason jars to put them in. And I love it. It brings me so much joy. It makes me feel rich and radiant to give something beautiful to someone else, and in doing that, it creates a ripple of delight that extends far beyond me.

On a larger scale, this has also shown up in how I think about legacy. There were things I had originally planned to leave in my estate, like scholarships, and at some point, I asked myself a simple question. *Why am I waiting? Why would I wait to give when I could do it now and be present for it?* So I decided to establish and endow scholarships while I am still here to experience them. I get to meet some of the women who receive them. I get to see the impact and be part of the story.

And then there are the moments that matter most, the ones that cannot be measured in dollars at all. Every Thursday, I spend time with my grandchildren. We call it Grandma Thursdays. That time is, without question, one of the richest and most radiant parts of my life. It costs nothing, but it represents everything. The space in my calendar, the freedom to choose how I spend my time, and the connection with the people I love most.

I have come to believe deeply in doing good, being grateful, showing appreciation, and living a legacy now, not later. That is my filter. It is the lens through which I make decisions. And when something aligns with that, it feels like a warm hug. It feels like an easy yes.

Improving your relationship with money and yourself begins now, shaped by the decisions you make today, the thoughts you believe, and the energy you bring into your life and into the lives of others. A rich and radiant life grows through the small, intentional moments you create and share. It shows up in the beauty you cultivate, the generosity you extend, and the quiet ways you brighten someone else's day, one bouquet at a time.

KEY TAKEAWAYS

- Being rich and radiant is a way of living, grounded in awareness, clarity, and vision that shape how you think, decide, and move forward.
- Your story about money matters, and shifting it toward possibility creates the energy needed to take consistent, aligned action.
- Simple, intentional systems and small daily choices build momentum over time, turning your financial plan into something steady and supportive.
- True alignment comes when your math, mindset, and soul work together, creating calm confidence, resilience, and ease in your financial life.
- A rich and radiant life is created in the present through generosity, meaningful experiences, and the small moments you choose to share.

EPILOGUE

"Just breathe. You are strong enough to handle your challenges, wise enough to find a solution to your problems, and capable enough to do whatever needs to be done."

— Lori Deschenes

Well done. Let me be the first to say, you are doing a great job showing up for yourself. And while I am proud of you, it is your future self who is the most proud. Because once you learn the simple steps to live a rich and radiant life, you cannot unknow them. You begin to see differently. You start to create decision filters. Living intentionally is no longer something you try to do; it becomes your lifestyle.

When you define freedom, fulfillment, and wealth for yourself, you step back into your power. Awareness, clarity, and vision propel your self-discovery. Mindfulness creates the space to access your inner wisdom, your splendor, so you can live a rich and radiant life regardless of your net worth. And from that place, your decisions become more aligned, more confident, and more you.

At the same time, it is important to recognize the cost of going back to old patterns. Avoiding your money mindset or staying on autopilot on a path that was never truly your choice slowly erodes your power. It delays your growth and robs you of your future wealth. You know too much now to hand that power back over.

So start by reviewing your "math of the moment." Simple binder paper works, and I have self-calculating templates that are easy to maintain if you want a system that feels supportive. Then take a deeper look at your money mindset. Write out your money story and edit it for facts. Ask yourself honestly if you like the results it is creating. If not, give yourself permission to upgrade it. This is a practice, and like any practice, it gets stronger with repetition.

From there, build your safety net and identify your "financial independence number," the number that makes work optional for you. Think of it as your GPS. It gives you direction, even if it evolves over time.

And just as important, find a community where you feel supported, where you can learn, share your wins, and celebrate others. There is something powerful about being in a circle where growth is normal and encouraged.

If this book has made an impact on you, share it. Share it with someone you care about. Share it with someone who needs it. Even better, bring this conversation into your workplace by sharing it with your HR department and introducing the idea of a Financial Wellness Workshop. This is how we widen the circle, one conversation, one person, one organization at a time. And there is always room in the circle.

As you continue forward, remember this: financial freedom is available to you. Your path may look different than someone else's, and that is exactly how it should be. When your journey aligns with your values and your desires, it becomes easier and more intentional. And in many cases, you will arrive there sooner than you expected.

You are capable of this. And you are already on your way.

ABOUT LIZ CARROLL

Liz Carroll is a lifelong student and teacher of making mindful money moves. Once believing she was "bad with money," Liz did the work to rewrite her money story, releasing limiting beliefs about how a woman can earn, spend, and save. That shift led her to financial independence and an early retirement from her corporate IT sales career.

Now, in her encore career, Liz helps women experience calm confidence with their finances by unpacking and transforming their own money stories. She brings order to chaos and clarity to confusion, illuminating the emotional side of personal finance with compassion and wisdom. Through her signature *Mindful Money Method*, a holistic blend of math, mindset, and mindfulness, Liz guides women toward lasting change through small, consistent actions that create freedom and fulfillment.

Liz is a Master Financial Coach (Ramsey Solutions), Certified Life Coach (The Life Coach School), and 200-RYT Yoga & Meditation Instructor (Purna Yoga College). She lives on the Oregon Coast with her husband, where their adult children and grandchildren visit often.

WHAT LIZ'S CLIENTS ARE SAYING...

"Before working with Liz, I felt like I was doing everything 'right,' working hard, living within my means, and saving consistently, but I still wasn't getting ahead. I didn't know how to invest or make my money work for me. I was stuck in a cycle of running faster just to stay in place. Deep down, I knew my mindset was part of the problem, but I didn't know how to shift it or what aspect needed to change. What I needed wasn't just financial advice; I needed holistic guidance that connected the dots between mindset, money, and long-term freedom.

I felt frustrated and discouraged, even a little angry. The help I needed wasn't something I'd ever been taught in school or shown along the way. This is life-changing information, and it felt unfair that it wasn't more accessible. I kept wondering, 'Why didn't I learn this sooner?' If I had, so many decisions would have been easier, and my life could have felt more enjoyable and empowered much earlier on.

So much has changed. At first, Liz helped me address the immediate, practical aspects of my finances, the tactical steps I hadn't known how to take. But the deeper shift came when we turned to mindset. Becoming aware of my beliefs about money, my self-worth, and my values brought everything into alignment. For the first time, I was able to approach my life as a whole rather than in disconnected parts. That unified approach has given me clarity, peace, and a deep sense of confidence. Now, every decision I make is grounded in self-awareness and aligned with what truly matters to me.

Because of the work I've done with Liz, I had the clarity and confidence to make a major cross-country move, a decision that not only advanced my career but also brought me closer to family at a time when they needed support. That move would have felt overwhelming before, but with the tools and mindset I developed, it felt aligned and purposeful. It's just one example of how our work together has empowered me to make big life choices with intention and trust in myself.

Liz is incredibly knowledgeable when it comes to everyday, practical financial matters, and she leads by example in her own life. But what truly sets her apart is her deep understanding of the mindset behind the money. She doesn't just help you manage your finances; she helps you understand yourself. She has a gift for helping people become aware of their thoughts and how those thoughts are shaping their outcomes. She provides the tools to shift those patterns, but always with compassion and respect for your pace.

Liz is all about helping you grow into the person you want to become and does so with encouragement, presence, and the gentle reminder that you're worthy of grace and space along the way."

– Debra Amorde, Maple Grove, MN - Content Operations

"During a period when I felt directionless and powerless, Liz helped me shift my thoughts, beliefs, and actions, leading to real results. When you change your mindset, all the opportunities in your life that you have wanted reveal

themselves. Working with Liz feels like a warm hug, and I always look forward to our sessions.

I moved into my dream house, am in a relationship with my soulmate, and I feel confident about my finances and the direction of my life.

If you go all in, so will Liz, and the results will transform your life."

– Courtney, Los Angeles, CA

"Transitioning from full-time corporate income to semi-retirement and not knowing what my financial resources really were, I was not confident in my ability to meet any financial challenges that might arise. After working with Liz, I know what my financial resources are. I'm confident in my ability to meet unexpected expenses, and I am mindful about aligning my spending with my values.

Last year was a masterclass in values-based living, where my financial freedom served as a tool for profound personal and relational investment. By removing financial concern from the equation, I transformed 'spending' into a series of intentional legacies in stewardship, relational abundance, and spiritual and physical endurance.

If you are on the fence about working with Liz, do it. My life is so much more abundant, and I mindfully live in alignment with my values as a result of my work with Liz."

– Margaret Hill, Portland, OR - Semi-Retired

"Before working with Liz, I lacked confidence in building my own business, and often felt overwhelmed and paralyzed by the next move. I now have a calm confidence in acknowledging my power. I have grown my business, career, family, and wealth in the last 5 years of working with Liz.

Take the leap of faith in her and in yourself. Reading this book feels like sitting across from Liz; calm, clear, and reassuring. Through significant life changes, career transitions, growing our family, and strengthening our financial health, Liz's steady presence has helped me slow down, think more clearly, and move forward with confidence rather than fear. Over time, her voice has become the one I hear when unhelpful or unproductive thoughts creep in, the voice that reminds me of my own power, calls me back to intention, and reframes money as a tool for abundance rather than anxiety. This book represents her same grounding presence. Liz guides you in recognizing what's already working, what's possible, and how to move forward in a way that feels aligned with your life and goals."

– Kelsey Bailey, Denver, CO

"Back in 2020, I was looking for someone like me (married, kids, career, and investing) but ahead of me, a life mentor. I did not have a plan or design for my life, including career, business, or investing goals. I felt like I was going through the motions, the mindset of 'this is happening to me' versus 'I'm choosing this'.

Liz taught me that I always have a choice, whether it's as complex as a career, an investment, or a life decision, or as simple as a scarcity-versus-abundance mindset (which sometimes feels heavier than the 'complex' ones). Working with Liz, I've doubled my salary, negotiated a work environment for myself, paid down debt, and increased my net worth. I feel more present each day, calmer when a wave of uncertainty and fear comes up, and I am designing a life I truly love.

All of this has shown me that you don't have to figure things out alone. While discovering more about yourself can feel uncomfortable, you always have the choice in what you want to do or feel! Yeah, Liz!"

– Bostyn Brodine, Colorado, Project Management Contractor/ Real Estate Investor/Gym Owner

1"Prior to working with Liz, one of my biggest challenges was mindset. I wasn't fully operating from a place of abundance or confidence, especially when it came to making big decisions in my business. I was working hard and making progress in my business, but internally, I didn't always feel confident in my decisions. There was a lot of pressure around making the "right" choices, especially when it came to partnerships, growth, and the direction of the business. More than anything, I struggled with fully trusting myself. I found myself overthinking decisions instead of feeling grounded in my own judgment.

One of our very first calls was about partnerships. A close family member wanted to partner with me on a real estate deal, and I was struggling with what I was actually looking for in a partnership and whether I should say yes. Liz helped me step back and realize that I didn't have to say yes to every opportunity or every person who wanted to partner with me. That shift alone was incredibly empowering.

Through working with Liz, everything began to change. As she helped me gain clarity, confidence, and an abundance mindset, I was able to reconnect with my intuition and learn to trust myself and my decisions again. That shift was incredibly empowering and has had a lasting impact on how I lead and grow my business today. She helped me develop a much stronger abundance mindset and gave me the confidence to rethink how I structured deals. Instead of defaulting to partnerships, I created a private lending program to raise capital through loans. Liz helped me see that I truly had something valuable to offer investors and that it was okay to confidently ask people to invest with me while providing them with a strong return.

My mindset shift completely changed the trajectory of my business. What started as a small real estate investing operation has grown into raising several million dollars in private capital and building a portfolio of over 200 units. Liz played a pivotal role in helping me step into confidence, learn to trust myself again, and gain the clarity required to grow at that level.

The value of working with Liz goes far beyond strategy alone. She has a unique ability to help you see your blind spots, shift your mindset, and step into the level of leadership your business actually requires. She has a way of asking the right questions and challenging you in a way that helps you grow. Even now, Liz continues to push me to expand my perspective, reframe my thinking, and develop as both a business owner and a leader.

If you're considering working with Liz, my advice is simple: do it! The clarity, mindset shifts, and leadership growth you gain can completely change the trajectory of both your business and how you show up. I love Liz, and she has played a pivotal role in getting me to where I am today! I look forward to working with her for many more years to come."

– Brea Burger, Denver, CO, Real Estate Investor/Capital Raiser